À ma grande sœur

Pour Noël 94

Joyeux Noël oxox

Cathim Wattin

Riding Logic

Wilhelm Müseler as Master of the
Berlin Hunt, 1929.

PRENTICE
HALL PRESS
EQUESTRIAN
BOOKS

WILHELM MÜSELER

Riding Logic

Edited by
KURD ALBRECHT VON ZIEGNER

Translated from the German by
HAROLD ERENBERG

PRENTICE
HALL
PRESS

New York   London   Toronto   Sydney   Tokyo   Singapore

Simon & Schuster
Simon & Schuster Building
Rockefeller Center
1230 Avenue of the Americas
New York, New York 10020

First Edition © 1983 Methuen London Ltd.

Copyright by Paul Parey Verlag
New material © 1965, 1973, 1981 by
Paul Parey Verlag

Published in 1987 by Prentice Hall Press

First published in Germany in 1933
as Müseler: REITLEHRE
by Paul Parey Verlag,
Berlin & Hamburg.

This fifth edition originally published in the United
States by Arco Publishing, Inc.

13   12   11   10   9   8

Library of Congress Cataloging-in-Publication Data

Müseler, Wilhelm
Riding logic.—5th ed.
1. Horsemanship
I. Title   II. Ziegner, Kurd Albrecht von
III. Erenberg, Harold   IV. Reitlehre *English*
798.2'3   SF309   83-73045
ISBN 0-671-76492-6

Preface

Anyone can learn to ride, for riding is a skill. A skill can only be acquired by practice and experiment and never by slavish imitation. And once skill has been attained, attention should be paid to keep it at the highest level.

Riding is a thing of beauty and can be made into an art form. All of us would like to be considered artists, but the only ones who will achieve this are those who try sincerely to enter into a horse's mind and effect rapport with him by sympathy rather than brute strength. Sympathy or feeling is not an unnatural science: we can all develop it to a considerable degree. The aim in dressage is complete harmony between rider and horse – quite simply, beauty. Then the horse looks relaxed and at ease and there is nothing in his rider's demeanour to show the efforts he has had to make.

Contents

Contents

CHAPTER ONE

Training the Rider

It is essential that a horseman practises three aspects of riding equally: riding in the school, riding outside and jumping. If one of these activities is neglected or imperfectly mastered he will never attain mastery with his horse.

It is rare that, at the onset of his training, a rider will know exactly the direction his interest will take him at a later stage. He will be certain only that he wants to learn to ride. However, the initial steps for all riders are similar, whatever their ultimate goal.

It should take about thirty hours for an individual to acquire some skill in the three paces on a quiet, obedient horse. This may suffice for a person whose only wish is to ride once a week as a brief, healthy, outdoor activity. Another person will want to reach a higher standard of skill than this, and yet another will want to make it his profession. The first of these views a horse simply as a means of carrying him about, while the other two see riding as a goal, possibly even an art form. The more restricted the undertaking, the quicker is its realisation and therefore the person in whom ambition and competitive spirit combine to form the higher ambition will have to be prepared to devote much more time and application. True riding mastery can only be reached by the person who, for years and years, has each day kept his mind open to new ideas, and even he should always be prepared to admit that there is still much to be learned.

A rider's training can be divided into three aspects, *seat, feeling* and *influence*. It would be impossible to say that one of these elements is more important than the others because they are totally inseparable and dependent on each other.

It would be out of the question for someone initially to achieve a good seat[1] and then, at a later stage, the other two elements isolated from it.

In the very first lesson then, one is concerned not just with learning to sit but also with feeling and influence. It is often said that the seat is the foundation of all riding. That is not devoid of truth but the fact of the matter is that the rider's position will be totally dependent on the influence he wishes to impart, and both of these, seat and influence, are determined by the feel.

Clearly therefore a rider must, from the very start, learn how to 'feel'. He must acquire an awareness of whether he is sitting his horse comfortably and in a relaxed manner and whether his seat is secured by balance only. He must know how to go along with the horse's movements and how to influence by use of back muscles, weight, legs and reins. If a feeling for all this is not acquired, it will not be possible for the rider to sit well, i.e. with relaxation and suppleness. Rather he will hang on to the horse as best he can and that will do nothing for his riding. A seat of this sort is totally wrong and, even if it looks quite decent to some people, it will not do because it is lacking in feeling and is stiff.

There are many riders who are convinced that they have mastered it all: they overestimate their ability and underestimate the skills to be learned. When difficulties are encountered, the fault is never theirs, rather their horse's. When they wish to appear especially knowledgeable, they blame their mount's faulty conformation: such a fault, when it does exist, has nothing or very little to do with the problems. This is one reason why so many horses are badly schooled and quite often it is these who are said to be well schooled. Well-schooled horses are found as rarely as skilful riders. As every rider will at some time have to cope with problems, it is essential that he pays some attention − even if only hypothetically − to why a horse acquires bad habits and how they

[1]If a rider is described as having a 'good seat', this comment, which one might take to mean that he sits well, extends essentially to his 'feel' and 'influences'.

may be cured. Every person who sincerely wants to call himself a rider should consider well the following: 99 per cent of all horses have bad habits which are glibly called 'disobedience'. And 99 per cent of all riders have no idea how to cure their horses of such bad habits and make no effort to learn how to set about doing this. They may well have heard that one should make one's horse attentive to the aids, but they do nothing about it. Through neglect and completely unintentionally they confirm their horses in a host of bad habits. They do not take the trouble to consider if the application of the aids (see p. 69) is really as difficult as has been made out. They therefore never realise that it is much simpler and just as easy to learn as accommodating oneself to the horse's movements. But here, too, 99 per cent cannot manage this, nor can they sit deeply in the saddle because they have not learned how to brace the back. A child can work a swing and yet most riders cannot apply similar laws to a horse. Every rider should ponder this well and decide it would be as well for him to master this dark secret!

Learning to sit

Deliberately, no sketch is shown of a 'correct seat' as much too much harm can result from over-emphasising an ideal in purely graphic depiction.
  Balance
  Relaxation
  Following the horse's movements
cannot really be shown graphically, nor 'feeling' described. But this is not to play down the importance of a good seat: it is stressed by drawing attention to the essential elements.

2 The 'correct seat'.

People are often in error as to what is meant by a rider's 'seat'. This has less to do with relative limb position than with the way a rider
1 keeps a position in the saddle by balance alone
2 sits with relaxation and
3 has learnt to follow his horse's movements.
  Mastering these three requirements means that one sits well and attractively, is in control of the limbs and can use them as the changing necessities dictate, and can influence in the best possible way.
  The concept of a so-called regulation 'correct seat' is a dangerous one leading to an overvaluation of a prototype seat and doing more harm than good.
  There are more ways than one of sitting a horse and much may be learned from watching other riders but, just as a diagram of a correct seat would force a rider into attempting slavish

imitation, so would it be wrong for a riding instructor to instruct a pupil to sit in a 'prescribed' manner. This would lead inevitably to *stiffness* and that is the absolute cardinal sin! (See p. 18.) Yet the question, 'How does the rider learn to sit?' is extraordinarily important. It is not an easy one and it is not to be dealt with in a few words, yet its resolution supplies the answer to the two most frequently posed questions from beginners: 'Am I sitting correctly?' and, 'Where am I still going wrong?' In effect, each rider has to find his own answer to these two questions. For he alone can tell whether he is sitting *comfortably* and has acquired *feeling*, and whether he realises what is involved and what is meant by the three principles of *balance, relaxation* and *following the movements of the horse*. The disposition of the limbs follows naturally and not in a prescribed manner and is determined by the kind of influence which is to be exerted. Leg and hand position will not therefore be discussed in answering the question, 'How does a rider learn to sit?', but rather in connection with 'Influencing by legs and hands' (p. 33), and the position of the torso will be discussed in connection with 'Influences of the body' (p. 40).

BALANCE

Balance is the first essential for a rider to master. This and only this will enable him to sit securely on his horse: arms and legs are not used to this end. The body should rest vertically on the seat bones and fork, i.e. on three supporting points and in the lowest part of the saddle. Ideally the lowest part of the saddle should be in the middle and not to the front or back as is unfortunately often the case with ill-fitting saddles: the top sketch of those depicted in illustration 40 on page 106 shows a correctly placed saddle. Arms and legs play no part in balance proper, and will only play a part in this respect if a rider has totally lost his balance and is in danger of falling off.

The quickest way for a beginner to practise balance is for him to walk and then trot slowly on a horse equipped with side-reins and it is as

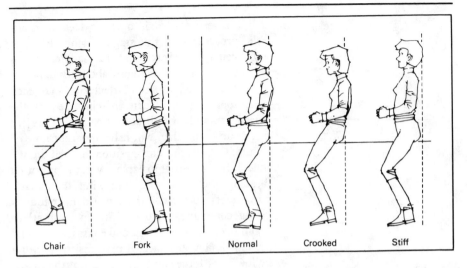

| Chair | Fork | Normal | Crooked | Stiff |

3 Various types of seat.

well if the instructor does not offer the rider advice in this phase so that he can concentrate on his task. The point of the side-reins is that the horse's movements are less pronounced and the rider is thrown about less in the saddle.

It is essential that the beginner be given a horse which moves smoothly and has a calm temperament. Stirrups should be used from the start, as they will make the rider feel more secure and he will quickly acquire confidence, relax and lose any stiffness. Should the beginner still have difficulties, the reason will probably be that his horse is too brisk in its paces: a change of horse is then recommended, for the easier the initial stages of learning are made, the quicker the beginner will become confident and learn balance.

When a measure of balance has been reached (and this should be after only a few lessons), it should be tested by having the rider dispense with stirrups, but this should be done gradually and not for too long a period in order to avoid a loss of confidence in the rider. A loss of confidence will inevitably mean that the beginner goes back to gripping with his legs and becoming totally stiff. A fall, too, is a set-back for the more timid rider, for he may well become apprehensive and revert to hanging on. It is advisable, then, for a rider to dispense with his stirrups as a gradual process – initially for a few steps – then to increase the periods once he feels comfortable, proceeding at this stage to look all round and even to do exercises in the saddle. In this way he will start to feel happy about his balance.

Balance is an aspect of dexterity that each rider soon grasps. It can be reinforced by the rider learning how to brace his back muscles (see p. 23) and only then will it be apparent how he should sit upright and position himself in the saddle. It is essential to explain what is meant by 'bracing the back' and 'following the horse's movements', otherwise there is a danger that in giving commands such as, 'Sit up straight' or 'Lean back', the pupil will make himself stiff and perhaps hollow his back. A person sitting with a hollow back forces his buttocks out of the saddle and to the rear and is then totally devoid of a secure seat through which he might hope to achieve balance.

Ideally one should try to achieve a balance that is automatic and instinctive, similar to that which is necessary when riding a bicycle. Only then can one begin to develop an ability to 'go with the horse' and accommodate oneself to its movements and also to learn how to influence by one's weight.[1]

The test of balance is when a rider maintains a secure seat without the use of stirrups in turning movements and serpentines with no tightening up or hanging on and when he, furthermore, can look all round from the saddle, move his limbs and converse freely. The achievement of all this is something best judged by the rider himself.[2]

Once a rider has learned to sit in equilibrium so that his horse can move freely, a point will be

[1]Riding bareback is useful here. The rider can sit on a blanket secured by a vaulting-girth and, if the horse has side reins, the rider can, by grasping the two handgrips of the vaulting-girth, bring his seat forward to the centre of gravity. In this position, with no fear of losing balance, he can relax the tensions in back and legs and feel the movements in the horse's back. This is without doubt the best way to 'connect' the rider's spinal structure with that of the horse.

[2]'Balance' and 'relaxation' are inseparably connected. But they are not identical terms. A rider must relax his muscles to the utmost degree in order to achieve balance. But it is not true to state that complete relaxation necessarily means a state of balance.

reached when the horse starts to make its own efforts to stay in equilibrium with his rider and it will then react closely to each and every displacement of weight just as a bicycle will when ridden 'without hands'. (See 'Body influence sideways', p. 45.)

It is important, too, for the more experienced rider to test himself from time to time by riding without stirrups. If it does not feel right, then it will inevitably be that the rider has a degree of stiffness that is affecting his balance adversely. Otherwise, it *would* feel right.

RELAXATION

By this term we mean a condition in which all limb joints are loose and muscles relaxed with no suspicion of involuntary stiffness. This is not to say that the rider's limbs may flop about. A conscious application of muscles is demanded just as it is in the case of a gymnast who performs gracefully on the bar, either balancing, vaulting or swinging.

The problem is that quite often a rider is in ignorance of whether his muscles are tight or not. It can be asserted, however, that stiffness is present if a rider is sitting in discomfort, maintains a required position only by exertion or hunches himself. Once a rider has attained a degree of balance, fear, stiffness and the tendency to hang on begin to vanish and a state of relaxation can begin.

It is often said that exercises carried out when sitting on a horse are useful in giving a rider confidence and helping his relaxation and balance. To look about from the saddle, move, converse, whistle and carry out exercises are beneficial in accustoming the rider to his horse and in making him relax, but only if he already has a degree of balance and the confidence that this bestows.

But far too many slogans are invoked without sufficient thought being given to them: a system is built on them and one finds time and time again that far too much time is wasted on such exercises. An excess of exercises may destroy balance. One can see frequent cases of a rider who possessed a decent relaxed seat reverting to gripping with thighs and legs after a surfeit of exercises such as mounted games.

Riding out does as much for relaxation and confidence as exercises and has the additional benefit that the rider gets to know his horse and the way it behaves. A foreign language is far better learned abroad than by learning the grammar at home from books. Once one has a working knowledge of a language, then is the time for rapid acquisition of grammatical fundamentals.

While much is heard of exercises on horseback, little attention is paid to exercises on foot. Poor bearing, bad carriage and stiffness will naturally adversely affect a rider's seat.

A differentiation may be made between postural faults which may look bad but nothing more, and faults that have an adverse effect. A similar differentiation should also be made between defects that are innate, such as bodily deformities or inadequacies, and those which have been acquired by bad habits, which may show when the rider is on foot and certainly will when he is on a horse. It is suggested that the instructor discusses such problems with the pupil, preferably not during the lessons. Where they originate from fear, from attempting too much or from too difficult a horse, the instructor and pupil can discuss what measures to take. But where the problems arise from bodily defects or bad habits all the instructor can do is to lay down a course of action which the pupil must follow closely.

In contrast then to exercising on horseback, exercising on foot when applied as a means of correcting a rider's faults of carriage and bearing must be tailored to the needs of each individual and not carried out by the class as a whole, each person's requirements being different from those of his colleagues.

The most frequently encountered problem is pain in the thighs caused by the unaccustomed stretching of thigh muscles. The person who continues to suffer from this will, in most cases, have subsequent trouble with his leg position. Only a person who feels comfortable in the

4 Henry Chammartin (Switzerland), Gold Medal winner, Tokyo 1964, riding Wolfdietrich. Suppleness, impulsion and a calm demeanour are the cardinal features in this beautifully ridden horse. He goes straight and obediently to his rider's imperceptible aids and is, at all times, ready to carry out the slightest command.

saddle is sitting well and in a relaxed manner. If a rider feels discomfort when sitting in the saddle, if he has trouble in keeping his legs just behind the girth without bringing his knee away from the saddle and if his legs do not, as it were, hang in a natural manner in that position, then he is, from a point of view of personal conformation, too narrow in the fork. This affects quite two-thirds of riders in the initial stages. The reason is invariably the strong but inelastic muscle structure of the inner thigh, something that is found frequently in adults.

When these riding pains cease, as they will do in the course of a few days, the rider still finds difficulties with his leg position without knowing why he is having problems. No amount of will-power, endeavours or strivings will prevent muscle stiffness returning if the legs are forced into the correct position. Exercises such as stretching each leg out sideways and straddling the legs wide apart can stretch the fork, or perhaps one should say the inner thigh muscles. But it must be emphasised that these exercises should be carried out several times each day – in the morning, in the afternoon and in the evening – if they are to have any beneficial effect. There is no other way of improving the thigh position or of relaxing one's legs than by this kind of exercising off the horse. And until such time as frequent leg-stretching and straddling exercises have had some effect, it would be as well if the pupil could ride a narrow horse with a not too pronounced action.

One must likewise try to combat positional faults and stiffness in hips and ankle joints, any rounding or lack of straightness of the back or uneven hips. Stiff wrists also need correcting, just as they would be in learning to play the piano or violin. It must be realised that it is just not possible to put all these points right in the relatively short time that a rider spends in the saddle. If he should neglect to follow his intructor's advice on their rectification, he must not be surprised in the slightest when his seat continues to lack those qualities of comfort, relaxation and good appearance and he continues to have difficulties with feel and influence. That is why it was stressed earlier in this chapter that, far too often, insufficient attention is paid to these exercises on foot. What is most damaging to relaxation is the advice riders are given as to seat corrections. That may sound ludicrous to outsiders. 'Surely you may tell a rider how to sit and make any necessary corrections!' But there is a logic at work here if one reflects. In the last analysis, seat corrections that are so often prescribed are nothing but enforcements into a predetermined shape, in other words, they destroy relaxation and lead to stiffness.

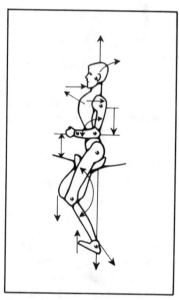

5 In effect, when a rider is forced into a predetermined 'correct seat' with no regard for any state of relaxation, he becomes nothing but a puppet, unable to feel or influence.

The position of body and limbs depends on the task they are to perform and the influences they are to bring about. For this reason it is folly to attempt to teach one a position in isolation: it should only be done with an eye to the way a rider will give aids and how he will be able to 'feel'. This is not to be taken as an indication that seat improvement is not important: far from it. It is of paramount importance, for it illustrates that only riding instruction in the widest possible sense can produce a seat such that a rider both feels what is going on and can influence correctly.

A half-halt should precede each activity – walking on, trotting on, coming to a halt, turning and cantering on. To ask for these half-halts, the rider should straighten his body, make himself longer and let his legs influence the horse. In doing this he will improve his seat and should, at the same time, be able to judge whether the half-halt has been totally effective and the horse has obeyed fully – but, for this kind of feel, it is essential that the rider himself be totally relaxed.

If rider and teacher pay close attention to the execution of these half-halts, which are of inestimable benefit to the acquisition of seat, feel and influence, seat correction as such will be quite superfluous. One should note well how frequently one must carry out a half-halt: it should automatically follow the instructor's call to attention before a command is given. It is immaterial whether the instructor watches what the class does in response to his call or whether he chooses to pay more attention to the attempt to obey his seat correction. But it is quite clear what the pupil has to do. He does not just do any one of the following: sit up straight, sit more evenly, push his chest forward, but simply asks his horse for a half-halt. That covers everything. Straightening oneself up is done for a particular purpose and must not be a matter of stiffening oneself. To ask properly for a half-halt, the rider has to combine making his body longer with straightening up, with bringing his legs inwards and being firmly in the saddle, with incorporating himself into the horse's movements and with an overall sense of 'feel'. A rider can only possess a good yielding seat when he has mastered totally the execution of a half-halt.

In contrast to the foregoing, individual items of advice on seat correction such as 'straighten up', 'sit evenly', 'chest forward' will only have the effect that the pupil makes his body stiff because he will concentrate on these different requests and try to execute them to the letter. It cannot be over-emphasised that what he has to do is to learn to *ride* and not to learn to acquire a model outline.

LEARNING TO FOLLOW THE HORSE'S MOVEMENTS AND SIT DEEPLY IN THE SADDLE

The problems begin in trotting on when a rider starts to be thrown upwards too much. Horses vary in the amount of movement they impart. The smoother the action, the more quickly the pupil comes to terms with being thrown upwards and his balance and relaxation improve rapidly. But should he subsequently ride his horse at faster paces, especially when side-reins are not used, or when he rides a different horse with more bounciness, he will suddenly find a great degree of discomfort.

The beginner may well seek to ameliorate this bumping by squeezing with legs or thighs. He will find this ineffective. It results in discomfort, in stiffness and in the horse rushing on.

The origin of this problem, which is, in effect, being behind the horse's movement, is dealt with in the section on body influence (p. 40). The sole remedy is to brace the back muscles. Bracing the back muscles is something that is done in an involuntary manner in everyday tasks, but because it is involuntary, few people have any idea of the role it plays in movements generally. The section that follows is meant especially for those who do not, since it is of vital importance and deserves thorough explanation. It is a fact that, even if one has grasped the idea of bracing the back, one may not understand its significance in riding.

Just as one can set a swing in motion by bracing the back muscles (illustration 8), one can make a horse move forward. Once a horse is moving forward, one can avoid similarly being left behind the movement: this involves accommodating oneself to the horse's movements or 'going with' the horse. If the idea of getting the horse to walk on has been properly mastered, one will be able to go along in harmony with it. But it is quite out of the question to do one of these things without the other. Many riders who have ridden for years have not grasped this prerequisite for a good seat which is totally necessary for the proper giving of aids. It cannot be neglected as something that may come by chance or will come 'in time'. It must be *practised* and *practised*. A well-schooled horse is essential in this for it will react immediately to back-muscle pressure. When the rider asks for walk on and uses not just his legs but also his loins and back muscles, he will find he needs very little in the way of leg pressure. The more a rider learns to use back muscles, the less he will need to urge with his legs. In asking for halt, the rider who uses his loins finds that the horse reacts very differently from the way he has halted previously. The rider when not using his loins can only ask for halt by pulling on the reins and this can often require quite a pull. Loin action ensures that the horse is impelled forwards into the bit, where, finding a resistance, it stops. It requires but little pressure for the horse to understand that it is not being asked to go on at a faster pace but to halt: the rider should get the feeling that his horse is lower behind and higher in front (see illustrations 29 and 48).

The best way for one to become conversant with the effect of back-muscle action is by repeated requests for walk on and halt and also frequent changes of pace, from halt to walk, from walk to trot, then back down to walk and halt. If one does not get the desired effect with one particular horse, one must ride other horses until one achieves success. Success has to be achieved, otherwise back-muscle action will never be learned.

It is obviously essential that a rider attains a feeling for the difference in the way a horse walks on or stops when asked to do these *with* and *without* back-muscle action. The difference is considerable. Only when comprehension is total can the rider perceive how such back-muscle action can prevent his being thrown up as severely as in the beginning.

At a gentle trot, the use of back-muscle action displaces the seat and centre of gravity forward in the saddle just as it does in walking on and halting and the consequence is that the position of the bottom of the spine is made secure. A rider sitting deeply in the saddle gives the impression of being almost part of it and fastened to it by the sucker effect of legs and back muscles. This may seem a totally strange concept to a beginner but, if he has the opportunity to sit on a well-schooled horse which has achieved self-carriage, he will feel immediately how it will seem to come to meet the rider's legs that should be hanging naturally along its sides. Close contact is thus established between rider and mount and the former does not need any particular expenditure of effort. It is advisable for either a well-schooled horse, or at least one that does not throw the rider upwards too greatly, to be used for the beginner to acquire the ability to 'go with the horse's movements'. Beneficial, too, are frequent changes of pace, for the back-muscle action that is called for in walking on and halting and then walking on again should be carried through into trotting. By using varying amounts of back-muscle pressure one can sit either deeply or lightly in the saddle without the *depth* of the seat being affected. The higher the horse's movement and the brisker the trot, the more back-muscle pressure must be applied. But as soon as a rider feels he has acquired the feeling for this, he must seek for the same result on other horses.

One can say one is 'glued to the saddle' when, on any kind of horse, one can sit at a strong trot without bumping in the saddle and, what is more, sit so securely that a piece of paper put under the seat will be held in place. Following the horse's movements is inevitably connected with flexibility and feeling: there is no room for stiffness or rigidity, for brute strength or great activity. An informed judge should therefore only be able to recognise this quality by the way the horse is going: he cannot do so by trying to observe what the rider is doing. The rider should be sitting calmly with no element of being thrown. Jerky and rippling movements of the back or a hollowed back are emphatically not the same as bracing the back. Sometimes in bracing the back a rider may lean backward a little, but it should not on that account be thought that leaning back is synonymous with back-bracing and one will not learn how to follow the horse's movement in this way. (See also illustration 48.)

The advice is often given that a rider should let his back 'swing along' with the horse. This advice is unsound, for following the horse's movements is not brought about by simply letting one's body swing with the horse, but by a conscious and deliberate muscular activity, a pushing forward of the body mass. The most useful analogy is that of a swing that is made to oscillate to a greater degree by bracing the back whereas it would gradually come to a position of rest if the person in it merely sat passively.

BRACING THE BACK

Bracing or applying the back muscles, in an equestrian context, is of the utmost importance in being effective and in giving aids, so much so that is hardly possible to give a proper aid if it has not been mastered.

One only knows how it feels when one has achieved success with it, and then only from a position of relaxation can one experience this special feeling. It is worth making the point that there must be no hint of stiffness in bracing the back. In practising this activity the rider is recommended to converse, whistle or sing if he

6
a: Normal seat
b: Braced back
c: Hollowed back (incorrect)

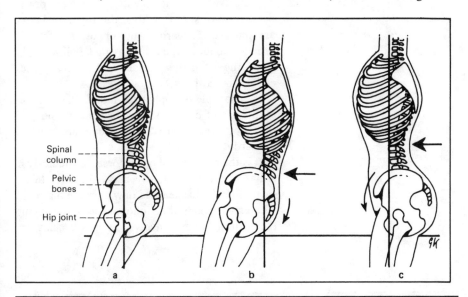

Spinal column
Pelvic bones
Hip joint

a b c

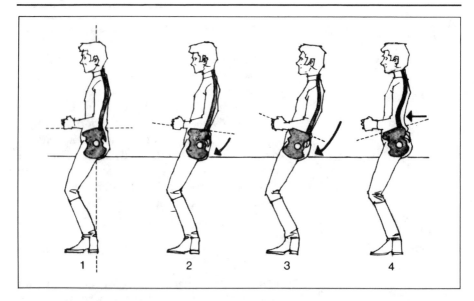

7
1: Normal seat
2: Braced back
3: Strongly braced back
4: Hollowed back (incorrect)

wishes. In fact he should do anything that will help him to avoid stiffening up.

In the normal position the spine curves in several places. One can verify this by feeling one's own spine and those of other people. In bracing the back, the lowest portion of the spine – that which includes the sacrum, the link between pelvis and spinal column – is displaced forward. This has the effect of pushing the rear of the pelvis back and down, and the front of the pelvis upwards and, in this, the two seat bones are pushed forward. The opposite effect is brought about by the rider having a hollow back. Here, the pelvis tips forward and the seat bones end up too far back.

It is possible to apply back-muscle pressure on both sides of one's body or just on one side, so that both seat bones or just one are pushed forward.

It is the reactions of one's horse, particularly if it has a soft and sensitive back, that will tell a rider when he has learned how to brace his back. The explanations that follow should clarify for the beginner what is involved in back-bracing.

Applying back-muscle pressure on both sides (pushing forward both seat bones):

1 On a swing, one braces the back to make the swing go forward and relaxes it for the backward movement (illustration 8).

8 and **9**

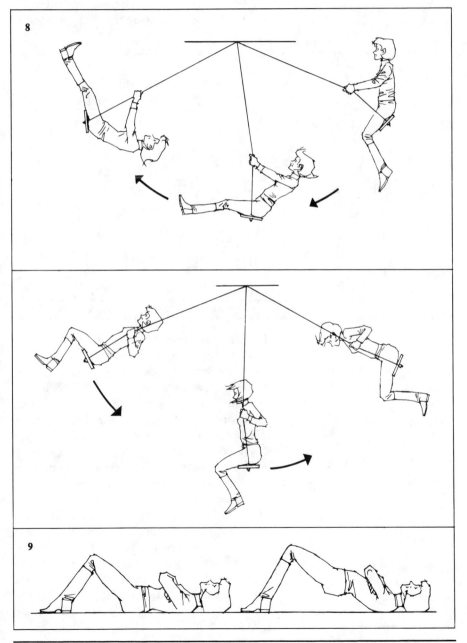

2 If one lies flat on the floor, one raises one's buttocks only by bracing the back muscles (illustration 9).

3 If one stands in front of a table with a book resting on the table but projecting from it and touching one's body, one can push the book wholly on to the table without use of the hands by bracing the back (illustration 10).

10

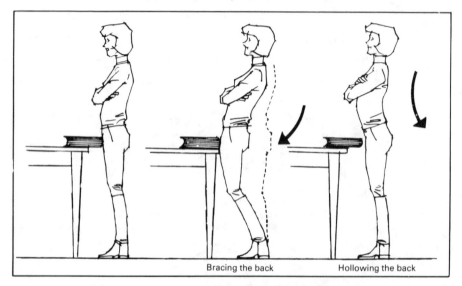

Bracing the back   Hollowing the back

This last example illustrates most clearly the difference between a *braced back* and a *hollow back*. Bracing the back pushes the seat forward, which is a requisite for riding, while hollowing the back forces the seat to the rear. Pushing the chest forward and bringing the shoulder blades together are a corollary of a hollowed back.

11

4 If one sits on a chair leaning against its back, thighs and buttocks can be made to slide forward by bracing the back.

5 If one sits on a narrow, light stool, one that is easily rocked, with legs apart, much as one might sit on a horse, one can tilt the stool forward by bracing the back. It is emphasised that the legs must not rest on the floor in front of the centre of gravity but be placed to left and right of it (illustration 11). If one sits on the front edge of a heavy chair, one can, in the same way, make it tilt.

However, it is not sufficient for a would-be rider to listen to these explanations and understand the illustrations. Understanding the movement is no substitute for *feeling* the action. It needs to be practised and when one feels one is mastering the art of back-bracing it must be practised on horseback until it can be done naturally and completely successfully (see illustrations 27, 28 and 29).

Bracing the back muscles on one side of the body (by pushing forward one only of the seat bones):

It is just as important to practise bracing the back muscles on one side of the body as the complete back-muscle structure. Achieving collection, turning and sitting at the canter can only be attained when the rider has learned to push forward his inside seat bone or hip. This must also be repeatedly practised until it can be carried out in a definite manner.

1 A swing can be made to move with a twisting motion by pushing forward one side of the body.

2 A person lying flat on the floor can choose to raise just one seat bone from the floor by bracing the appropriate back muscle.

3 A person standing in front of a table over the edge of which a book projects can, without using his hands, push the book in a twisting direction from one corner back on the table by using either his left or right back muscle.

It is no more difficult to practise bracing the back in the initial stages of riding than later on. The back muscles can be braced in varying degrees just like any other set of muscles and it is therefore obvious that aids may be given with infinite degrees of muscle action. One can push one's seat strongly forward or less so, or one can simply brace the back just enough to prevent the seat sliding backward: the back can equally be completely relaxed. But all this is part and parcel of the same exercise. It is stressed that repeated practising is essential: it is not sufficient to know about it intellectually.

It must never be forgotten that back-bracing is the foundation for a correct seat, for walking on and halting. Aids cannot be given without back-muscle action – a halt then becomes a matter of tugging at the reins. Without back-muscle action one cannot sit properly: if the seat is bad one cannot be effective. And on such a shaky basis one has no chance of correcting faults or disobedience in a horse.

The faults which occur in bracing the back are (see illustration 12):

1   The rider does not practise the movement sufficiently on foot, believing mistakenly that it is enough to have understood what will be required when he is mounted. However, when he is mounted he does not know how to use his muscles.

2   The rider does not concentrate on back-muscle bracing on horseback to the extent of mastering it. It can only properly be acquired when it is rigorously applied in each walk on, trot on and halt. And it must be borne in mind that the thighs must, at all times, be in contact with the horse's body.

If the rider does not succeed in these aims on one particular horse, he should change to another until it begins to feel right.

It is often said that a rider has a lot of back, that he has a definite back or that he has no back. These expressions are somewhat misleading. All horsemen are endowed with much the same amount of back, but they will not all apply it equally. In most people the musculature is of such a strength that it will not give way when unusual demands are made. Real back pains come into a different category. These may occur through the rider being thrown about at the trot, by riding for too long and similar over-exertions. However, such pains can rarely be attributed to too strong an application of back-muscle action and the pushing forward of the seat.

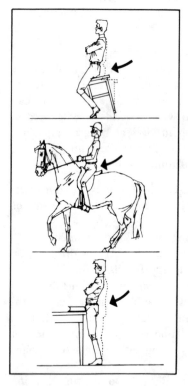

12 Bracing the back in asking for a halt (see also illustrations 27-29 and 47).

How does the rider learn to feel?

When one talks of a rider's ability to *feel* one understands his ability, at all times, to judge how well he is sitting, his effectiveness, his giving of aids and equally, as far as his horse is concerned, its responsiveness, its degree of collection and whether it is paying attention. This sense of feeling should tell a rider how his horse is going, when action or an aid is necessary and with what degree of firmness; then quick judgement as to whether what he did was effective and the intention achieved or whether the action should be repeated.

Feeling is something that one has to teach oneself. Teachers can only try to stimulate it by good instruction, advice on self-discipline, appropriate lessons, and the way they react to the manner in which the pupil tries to carry out their commands. The type of lesson is relatively unimportant: what is important is the manner in which it is carried out.

Critical self-examination will be demanded constantly after each request for the giving of an aid or an influence or after a lesson: only in this way and by the individual realising what is wanted can feeling be awakened and fostered. Feeling can best grow in a climate in which a beginner starts with and masters easy tasks before he is confronted with the more difficult ones.

Should a rider struggle in vain to master a difficult request, he should not content himself with an inferior performance – this blunts one's striving for feeling – but ask his instructor for help. No instructor worthy of the name would take such a request amiss. But he would certainly take exception to a pupil trying to deceive him: he would consider such an attitude indicative of lack of commitment and would give that pupil less of his time in the future. Keenness shown by a pupil is invariably a stimulus to a teacher and vice versa.

An example will illustrate this point. The instructor asks for a halt (see p. 115), requiring the rider to make simultaneous use of back, legs and reins. The rider fears that, if he uses extra leg pressure, his horse will not give him halt but go on at an increased pace. He therefore omits leg-influence and merely applies pressure on the reins. Very many riders have thought of the instructor's requirement as involving a contradiction, but have never taken the trouble to ask for an explanation. This is very wrong. The pupil should discuss things with his instructor and then try the halt on a different horse or on other, better-schooled horses until he can really execute this movement. It is a sad fact that the horse is often blamed for lack of success, but the truth of the matter is that continually carrying different riders quickly dulls a horse's edge, even when the riders are good. It is simply out of the question to keep it at a pitch one would desire and, for this reason, one may not get the feel that is required on a particular horse at a particular time. But if one has learned to give correct aids on a well-schooled, sensitive horse, then a lesser-trained horse will react correctly to them. As the striving for feeling develops, it becomes increasingly important to ride different horses as each horse gives a different response from others. This obliges the rider to re-think his views on feeling and enlarges his ability to give aids tailored to the differing sensitivities of different horses.

It is the horse which is undoubtedly the best and only master of the art of giving the rider a sense of feel. Patiently and untiringly it can tell its rider where he is going wrong. One has only to interpret its reactions and make corresponding corrections. Such reactions are experienced most frequently by beginners and they are not backward in labelling their horse a useless creature which is stiff, devoid of feeling and insensitive.

The reactions that a horse manifests are of various kinds. Head-tossing is traditionally one of the horse's heartfelt cries: 'Don't pull my mouth about so much!' Kicking out with the hind feet towards the rider's legs means, 'Don't tickle me with your spurs!' Swishing the tail means, 'Your legs are too noisy: you're annoying me with your spurs!' Pulling means, 'Your hands are too unyielding!' In point of fact the horse pulls only as hard as the rider's hands. Life teaches us that pressure produces a counter-resistance. When a rider complains that his horse has a hard mouth he is, in effect, condemning his own lack of skill. It is beyond dispute that many horses develop a hard mouth with little apparent feeling in it through being tugged about continually. But if one adopts a more sensitive and softer approach to riding them, then the hardest mouth will begin to feel softer in a very short space of time. When the question of feeling is under discussion, most riders think initially of their hands, but it is most important that they learn this business of feeling through their seat rather than through the hands. The best illustration of this may occur for the beginner in his very first stages of instruction when his horse comes to a halt but does not put one hind leg down or has it behind the other one. This usually occurs after a full halt and the beginner will get the sudden feeling that he is sitting lower on one side than on the other. But he does not know how this has happened. Very often one can observe him shifting about to try to achieve a level position: he sits up, stands in the stirrups, sits down again and in the end gives it up as a bad job. His fiddling about in the saddle has had no effects so he forgets all about it. But all the rider needed to do was to apply gentle leg pressure which would allow the horse to rest all four legs evenly on the ground and he would then find that he was sitting evenly, since the lower side of the horse had become higher.

This example should bring home to the reader the importance of taking note of what may seem trivial and not leaving it to the instructor to discover all the problems. Feeling will only be learned by the person who *uses his brain* and interprets what he feels.

Applying this, the rider himself is the best judge of whether he has learned to 'go with the horse's movements', for he should *feel* himself bumping about in the saddle and can form a judgement as to whether he can remedy it. If a rider has not acquired feeling to the extent that he can retain a sheet of paper between his seat

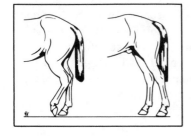

13 An early opportunity to feel what the horse is doing: here (left) it halts resting one foot, or (right) it takes a step back with one foot.

and the saddle, then he should not be paid the compliment of having 'a good seat' or 'a good leg position' and he should be the first to acknowledge that he still has to master the most important aspects of sitting. Many riders, among them people who have been riding for a considerable time, when asked to answer truthfully, would have to admit that they would not know when their horse was cantering on the wrong lead. If a rider does not feel this incorrectness in the very first canter stride, then he is sitting badly and not going with the horse's movements.

There are also very few riders who have a proper comprehension of what is meant by the expressions 'on the bit', 'obeying the aids' and 'behind the bit'. These are so important that they will be discussed in detail in 'Making a horse obedient to the aids', pp. 69–74.

A good way for a rider to form his own judgement of what he has learned is for him to ride sensitive horses.

This enables him to check that:
on a horse with a sensitive back, he can follow its movements smoothly,
on a horse with a light mouth, he has a yielding hand,
on a ticklish horse, his legs are quiet.
The more sensitive the horse, the more searching the test will be for the rider.

Most riders, however, are complacent and prefer not to put themselves to such tests, or if they do and are found wanting, put the blame on the poor horse. They feel indignation that their ability is called into question.

Feeling can only come through practice and it is consolidated by continued practice, but only if one is prepared to make efforts. Without personal involvement and discipline, in other words self-examination and positive thinking, no one will learn anything.

How does the rider learn to influence?

A rider can influence his horse by using legs, reins, his weight and back. Logically,
the legs are a driving force,
the reins restrain,
the weight is used in turning movements,
while the back is essentially a connecting link for these various motive forces.
We shall discuss these influences separately.

The degree of application of these various influences is determined by the relative sensitivity of the horse. But none of them should be applied with such force that the horse is given a physical goad or stimulus. When one uses various influences together, one is in the position of being able to call on an infinite number of gradations of influence and effect. These combinations, the medium through which the rider tells his horse what is required of him, are called *aids*. There are different aids for walk on, for trot, for canter, for turning right and left, for halting and so on (see Chapter Three, The Lessons, p. 114 and following). Each of these aids consists of several influences which all have to be imparted simultaneously if the horse is to understand what the rider requires. One does not talk therefore of leg-aids and rein-aids but of influencing with the legs, influencing with the reins and so on.

One might think that it would be useful for the rider to practise the influences one by one and then, when he has mastered them, to apply them in the giving of aids. Unfortunately this does not work, for the horse will only react properly to influences when they are given together: only then do they make sense to the horse as aids. To take an example, if one wishes to try out what effect tightening the reins will have without accompanying this by using the back and legs, the horse will have no idea what is expected of it. Certainly it may raise or lower its head, yield to or fight against rein pressure, throw its head about, in fact most things save the important one – knowing what its rider requires.

It is essential, then, that the rider learns from the very onset to give correct aids. He should therefore begin with the most elementary aids: the ones for walk on, trot and halt. These aids are the easiest to give because they require the rider's influences equally on both sides of the body without any displacement of weight being necessary.

More difficult aids are those which demand that the rider uses leg or rein influences on one side more than on the other. For this reason they are best practised at the halt, for the inexperienced rider, while his horse is in motion, is still coping with problems of balance as he has not yet mastered an ability to go with the horse's movements and he tends to stiffen up when called upon to influence on one side only of the horse's body.

A quiet school horse will turn at the corners of the school without any prompting from its rider even when it has side reins and this will show the rider how to move his weight to the inside but will not show him how to give a turning aid. Turning on the forehand and on the hindquarters are therefore indispensable preparatory exercises (see pp. 126 and 128). In these, the rider can learn in step-by-step manner how to apply his influences carefully one after the other so that the horse is in no doubt as to what is wanted. And what the rider learns in this way will form a basis for all further lessons. The smaller and less perceptible the aid, the more profound is the relationship between rider and horse.

LEG INFLUENCE

Sensitive leg influence requires the heel to be kept down: this is also beneficial in giving a deep seat and deep knee position and in tensing the calf muscle. The lower legs work in the following way: they drive forward when placed close behind the girth, and this the beginner notices very early in his training when he finds that a horse, from rest, will go forward when pressure from both legs is applied or repeated pressure is applied; when applied about a hand's breadth behind the girth, they can provoke a sideways movement or prevent a sideways movement if it has not been asked for – this, too, is something the beginner will experience early on, when, on coming to a halt, his horse has the inside hind leg off the track due to the rider's uneven leg influence, and this the rider can correct by pressure from the inside leg.

A rider's leg, of course, exerts influence on the horse's hind leg on that side. In time the use of leg influence refines itself to the degree that it becomes automatic and the rider does not need to think about it or when to apply it. Likewise the amount of application of the influence is given as a matter of instinct.

The sensitiveness of the horse will determine whether a rider needs just leg pressure or a succession of pressures and how hard is the necessary application. One talks of the driving influence of the legs but it must be noted that they do not constitute a driving force that a horse cannot resist. A young horse needs to be taught the significance of leg influence with reinforcement with the whip. And any horse can grow stale and refuse to obey the legs and even 'throw' itself against the leg. It is then important that influencing with the legs be made smoothly and always in the same way and, for this, it is essential that the legs are always in a relaxed and steady position.

Leg position
The legs should be in constant light contact with the horse, with the rider able to feel the warmth of the horse through the calves of his boots.

The legs must not be too far out to the side. One would then have to move them too far when being obliged to use them, which would surprise and frighten the horse. A noisy leg irritates a horse just as much as a varying rein contact.

The legs should not be pressed firmly round the horse's body, for they would grow tired and the horse would be totally unresponsive to any light pressure. When it is necessary to apply leg pressure it should be done swiftly and with only a slight degree of increased pressure. The rider urging his horse along with tremendous leg grip is a fiction of the writers of Westerns. One applies as little pressure as is necessary: it is less tiring and the horse appreciates it the more.

A rider's leg position should not be uncomfortable or inconvenient and should be as natural as possible. This is not at all easy for the novice rider and exercises are useful in this connection. Forcing oneself or placing oneself into set positions acts against a natural, relaxed posture and leads only to stiffness.

There is no set angle to be made between leg and thigh as length of leg differs so considerably and the roundness of the horse's body has to be taken into account. The longer one's legs and the narrower the horse's body, the more acute the angle will be: the shorter the rider's legs and the broader the horse, the more obtuse the angle will be. Obviously, then, a rider will adjust the length of his stirrup leathers to conform with the kind of horse he is riding.

Stirrup-leather adjustment
One can make an approximate adjustment of stirrup-leather length with the arms before mounting, but precise adjustment must then be made from the saddle.

Stirrups are too long if one has to depress the toes to reach the stirrups or if one cannot keep a contact with the horse's sides.

They are too short when the legs are forced too firmly against the horse's sides, which makes leg movement difficult. This is caused by the short stirrups raising the lower leg and knee, which has the effect of pushing the seat backwards from the deepest part of the saddle. The rider thus loses the secure foundation for his seat and he grips with his legs.

With the correct length of stirrup, the legs can be used freely and can be kept in light contact with the horse: furthermore, with toes raised the stirrup irons hang vertically under the soles of the feet, which is convenient if one has lost one's stirrup inadvertently. Care must be taken that the stirrup leathers are not twisted and lie flat along the calf. A twisted leather interferes with one's ability to feel and makes it easier to lose a stirrup.

The rider should have the ball of the foot on the stirrup iron, which allows him full use of the ankle joint. He should try to put pressure on the inside of the sole of the foot on the stirrup so that the outer edge of his sole is somewhat higher than the inside edge. This will give the thighs a flatter position and make the knees deeper. For hacking out, the stirrup leathers should be shortened by two or three holes and for jumping higher obstacles three to five holes. At a racing gallop, they should be even shorter, with the feet right into the stirrup irons.

Knee position

The knees should be as low or deep as possible. This is not because the knee has a role to play in influencing, but because the way the thighs will rest is dependent on the height of the knees, as is the position of the seat. One should have the thighs and legs in as much contact with the horse's body as possible. If the knees are drawn up too high, the thighs are too near the horizontal and the seat is displaced to the rear (chair seat). The rider must learn to judge his knee position and be able to lower the knees. When riding in a flexed position, in all turning movements and at the canter, the inside knee and heel must be kept well down. This can only be done if the rider has brought his ability to 'feel' to a sufficient degree. If one wishes to brace the back on both sides, one needs to bring both knees downwards (see p. 24): if the back is to be braced on one side only, then the inside knee only is lowered. The action is simply a matter of using both or just one of the seat-bones, for, to some extent, the same muscles are used. If the rider has attained mastery of this, he will not find it difficult simultaneously to lower his knees.

However, there are limitations to be noted in lowering the knees:

1 The lower legs must not lose contact with the horse, something that can easily happen with a long-legged rider on a small horse.

2   The legs must not be drawn too far back: they should lie on the girth where they can drive.

3   One must avoid losing the firm base provided for the seat by the three supports – the two seat bones and fork – otherwise a 'fork seat' results.

Knee grip

Knee grip is a term used for the firm pressure of the knee lying close to the horse's body.

The knee is a joint allowing movement of the lower leg and it is essential that one be able to move it freely. Therefore it will seldom be pressed hard against the horse's flanks. This would act against its full use. Only in exceptional cases should a rider grip with the knees to give him support when he has shortened his stirrups and something unexpected has happened. Consequently knee grip is used especially by riders when racing and jumping. Riders who have achieved a good measure of relaxed balance in their seat can practise gripping with the knees in the rising trot without reins.

14 William Steinkraus (USA) riding Sinjon XX. The considerable success achieved by the American teams can be attributed to a consistent training pattern and attention to style.

The toes

The toes should be angled slightly outwards. This position should follow naturally. If they pointed straight towards the front, the rider, when wanting to apply increased pressure, would find his calves sliding upwards along the horse's sides and his attempt to influence would be unsuccessful. If one were to point the toes outwards at a right-angle, one would find the lower legs would involuntarily clamp themselves against the horse and be totally useless from the point of view of influencing.

If a rider has to ask other people if his leg position is a good one, he has no 'feel'. It is necessary that this self-judgement be cultivated, for only the rider himself knows whether his leg position is comfortable, if his stirrup leathers are the right length, if he is able to keep his stirrups and if he is keeping in light but constant contact with the horse's body so as to be able to influence meaningfully at any required time.

Even the most experienced rider should ask himself frequently whether his 'feel' is up to the mark: it is easy to deceive oneself. Beginners should note that for this reason even expert riders will, from time to time, ride for a period without stirrups.

A similar question should also be asked as to whether one has a true light contact with the horse or whether one is imagining it. This can be done by using the leg on one side to influence the horse's quarters to take half a step to one side, and then the leg on the other side so that the horse takes half a step with his quarters to his other side. This may be carried out at the halt or in motion. Such small movements are required for this that they should be imperceptible to an onlooker. But the rider will know whether his 'feel' is up to standard, for, if he has to make a big movement with his legs, this will mean he had them too far away from the horse with no possibility of achieving his intention by a subtle increase of pressure. The more one practises this, the more the feeling for it will grow.

BODY INFLUENCE

The seat in a position of equilibrium
Every body, whatever its shape, has a centre of gravity or centre of mass. If the centre of gravity is supported, the body is said to be in equilibrium. The vertical line through a centre of gravity is called a line of gravity. Each body has only one centre of gravity and only one vertical

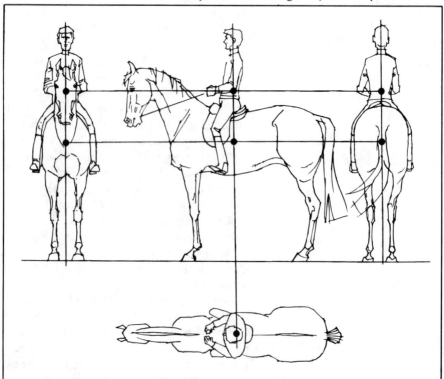

15 The seat in a position of equilibrium. The heavy black dots denote centres of gravity.

line can be drawn through it at any one time. A body can have several supporting points, for example a table has four legs (as a horse has) or three legs (as a rider has who is supported by his seat-bones and fork). As we have said, if the centre of gravity is supported, the body is in equilibrium; if it is not, it will topple over. If a body changes its shape (as happens in a living body when it makes a movement), the centre of gravity takes up a new position. The centre of gravity may even lie outside the body's mass, as with rings, hollow balls, bowls, or as with a rider in a jumping or racing position.

A rider sitting correctly has his centre of gravity vertically above that of his horse. His line of gravity coincides with his horse's, assuming that the horse is standing evenly on all four legs on level ground.

Each movement of the horse (stretching or raising the neck or head) and each lateral movement to left or right displaces the centre of gravity to a greater or lesser degree. The rider must seek to keep his own centre of gravity above that of his horse: in other words he must achieve a balance. This may sound like boring theory but it is fundamental to all 'feel'. Harmony cannot be attained without it and neither can that which we call 'a rider sitting in a position of equilibrium'.

When the rider is in this state of balance, the horse is able to give of his best and the rider can give his best instructions to the horse. After all, a porter carries a case on his back in a state of balance, and perhaps one best observes the laws of balance in the performance of a juggler.

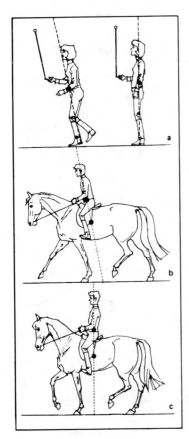

16 Centres of gravity:

a: A juggler

b: In the forward seat (half-seat)

c: Normal seat (with rider sitting fully in the saddle).

Balance when moving forward

When a horse moves forward, its rider must, depending on the speed of the movement, move his own centre of gravity forward in advance of that of the horse, if he wishes to keep his seat by balance. This is called 'going with the horse' or 'following the horse's movements' (see p. 20). If the rider stays behind the movement, he will only keep his seat by gripping with his legs.

There are two requirements that the rider should fulfil:

a His centre of gravity should always be in accord with that of the horse;

b His seat must have as its base the three support points – the two seat-bones and the fork.

There can be problems in reconciling these two requirements. In the forward movement, the appropriate displacement of the centre of gravity can only be achieved by inclining the upper body forwards. This involves a raising of the seat-bones and the rider finds himself seated on his fork only and will seek extra support from his reins and thighs (forward or half seat).

At a slow tempo in the short paces (walk – collected trot – collected canter), this irreconcilability is not so evident: it is present though and makes it difficult for the beginner to 'go with the horse'. The crucial moment is inevitably at the start of a pace when the rider, in a position of inertia, tends to lurch over backwards.

The aid for 'walk on', and this applies to other paces, is then inextricably connected with the need for bracing of the back and with leg pressure (see p. 115), identical means through which the rider sits securely in the saddle and goes with the horse's movement. A rider who is urging his horse forward is, metaphorically speaking, anchored in the saddle with legs and loins and is pushing his seat-bones and centre of gravity forward. This puts him in the closest contact with the horse so that he bounces less in the saddle and is not left behind the movement. He should still be sitting securely on his three support points; he should be in a perfect position at any time to influence his horse, stop, turn or urge it forward; he will stay in the saddle even if his horse stumbles; if the horse stops or shies he can push it on again; in short, he is controlling his horse.

In a forward seat (half seat) a rider is not really on the horse's back. His upper body is inclined forward and he is not sitting squarely on his seat-bones: if, then, the horse stops or stumbles, his only remedy to avoid being thrown out of the saddle is to increase his knee pressure, something that is tiring. If he should wish to influence in any way, he must first take up a correct seat again. The practised rider can take up such a seat again in a split second without disturbing the rhythm of his horse because he has learned to go with the movement of his horse. But the person who has not acquired the art of sitting totally deeply in the saddle will never master the ability to give aids while in the forward seat.

At fast paces, the problem mentioned of keeping one's seat securely on its three supports and the need to keep the centre of gravity in accord with that of the horse becomes a much greater one. It results in the rider having to do a rising trot when he would like to do a sitting trot but cannot accommodate himself to the horse's pace. At a brisk canter he has to lean right forward and when the pace is faster still, he has to abandon his seat in the saddle and adopt a position in which he is out of the saddle (see p. 156), for otherwise he would be incapable of following the movement and would impede the horse. In such a case he will find support with knee pressure, shorter stirrup leathers and resting his hands on the horse's neck.

It should be noted that the correct seat in both jumping and racing does not contradict the requirements of the classical riding doctrine of balance and harmony.

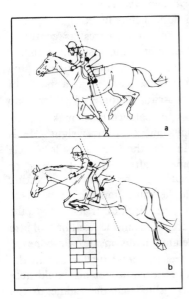

17
a: Racing seat
b: Jumping seat.

Body influence when moving forward and backward

Does a rider inclining his body forward or backward exert any influence on his horse? As mentioned, the forward movement of the horse requires that the rider follow its movement, but it should be noted that the rider moving his centre of gravity forward or back has no appreciable influence on the horse.

The reason is this: the rider, in leaning forward or backward, gives up largely the secure foundation on which his seat depends, either seat-bones or fork, and this changes involuntarily the ability of his back and legs to influence. Such a change has its consequences and it obscures the effect of displacing the weight.

It might be assumed that a simple leaning forward would tend to urge a horse on. This is not so: while a rider is obliged to incline his trunk forward at the faster paces, he cannot make a horse go faster by such an action.

Similarly, one might think that leaning back and therefore displacing the centre of gravity to the rear would have a restraining effect on the horse. But it often brings about a driving-forward effect because the rider tends to brace his back while leaning back. A simple relaxed leaning back, however, unaccompanied by muscle action, will have no such driving effect.

Balance in the sideways movements

The moment a horse bends its body to right or left, flexes or turns, it displaces its centre of gravity by an amount commensurate with the degree of movement. Additionally, when turning at any speed, the horse leans in as a means of counteracting centrifugal force. A rider who wishes to remain in balance must make a corresponding displacement of his weight. He is helped in this in that the horse's inside muscle structure becomes flatter when it flexes or bends. This means that the rider who is sitting deeply in the saddle will automatically be made to lean towards the inside. If he now puts increased pressure on his inside heel, he will also increase the weight on his inside seat-bone. A rider begins to feel the necessity for this in the very early stages of learning, for he should note some tendency to slip from the saddle to the outside when his horse is turning unless he leans in like a cyclist. However, it must not be assumed from this that simple leaning inwards of the upper body will allow one to achieve the desired shifting of the centre of gravity. The rider will probably collapse at the hip-joint, engendering entirely the opposite effect to what is required.

If the rider wishes to remain as one with his horse, with legs in close contact and with a constant rein contact, he must, depending on the extent of the horse's bend, keep his hips and his shoulders parallel with those of the horse.

The legs control the horse's quarters and take up, of their own accord, a correct position if they are in light, close contact with the horse – the inside leg on the girth and the outside leg a hand's width behind the girth.

The rider's hands similarly make a small turning movement in the same direction as the hips. This will allow the inside hand to come back somewhat and the outside hand to go forward by the same amount. Thus the horse's neck is always pointing straight forward when

18 The seat in equilibrium, showing displacement of weight to one side.

viewed from the saddle and, to an observer giving a quick glance, the rider will appear to be sitting perfectly straight.

When riding a small circle, the horse slopes in rather more. The rider's centre of gravity should now not be exactly over that of the horse but rather more to the inside in order to counteract centrifugal force.

The bringing forward of the outside shoulder is shown clearly in illustration 57.

A simple check for the rider to establish whether he is sitting in a position of equilibrium is for him to take his feet out of the stirrups in the turn and stretch his lower legs away from the horse. If he starts to slip towards the outside he is sitting badly.

Body influence sideways
The horse's weight-carrying area is much less left to right than from front to back. It follows then that, with the centres of gravity of horse and rider coinciding, the former will feel the slightest deviation sideways of the latter's body. The rider can therefore deliberately move his centre of gravity to influence the horse to make a similar movement of his centre of gravity. This is called influencing by the body. If body influences are carried out properly, they are almost imperceptible to the average observer: an exaggerated movement is one that is badly executed.

'The horse takes up a position that conforms with that of his rider.' If one turns this round and states: 'The rider should take up a position that conforms with that of his horse,' this will hold good as regards the rider's seat and position in all turning movements, work on two tracks, collected paces and at the canter. True harmony stems from the feeling of oneness that should exist between rider and horse. Only from a position of this harmony can natural aids be given and the ability to ride with an absolute minimum of effort be cultivated. This is why the performance of a dressage rider does not drop off as he gets older: he should improve.

Any displacement of weight to right or left causes the horse either to deviate from his pre-

19 Half-pass to the right at trot. The horse is flexed to the right and moves forward and sideways without losing rhythm and impulsion. This is an ideal performance. Both rider and horse are perfectly together. Frau Marg. Tengelin (Sweden) on Red Reve (see also illustrations 67-69).

20 The Spanish Riding School, Vienna. Shoulder-in to the right at the trot. Each diagonal pair of legs moves simultaneously, the inside (right) hind into the same spot as the outside (left) fore. The horse is flexed to the right.

vious course or to bend his body towards the appropriate side (see illustration 20 – 'shoulder-in'), depending how back, reins and legs have been used.

It cannot be over-emphasised that any shifting of one's weight must be so slight that, to the

layman's eye, one is simply sitting. Too pronounced a movement is to be avoided at all costs.
If one can be seen to have shifted one's weight,
one has overdone it and the performance was
bad.

REIN INFLUENCE

People talk much too much of influencing with
the hands or using the reins. Most riders are
inclined to do far too much with their hands.
Most people think they can use their hands well
enough because they have to use them in normal
daily life. Some people cannot even talk without
using their hands.

It is often said of a rider, 'He has good hands.'
A rider's hands can only be called good when
they are quiet and that is only possible if he can
sit calmly and deeply in the saddle, understands
how to brace his back, can go with the horse's
movements, and, most important, knows how to
urge his horse sensitively forward up to his controlling hands and thus be effective. One should
therefore rather praise his overall performance
than speak of his hands in isolation. The influence of the hands is important but to nothing
like the extent it is usually thought to be.

The lighter a rider's hands, the more complete
his mastery will be. Over-strong use of the hands
is a besetting sin.

Women, who lack the bodily strength of their
male counterparts, invariably have better hands
than men.

A rider can only make meaningful use of his
hands if he isolates them from any activity into
which his body may be impelled by jolting or
suchlike. This can only be achieved if upper
arms and forearms, muscles and joints are totally
relaxed.

With someone who has not acquired a degree
of balance, it is advisable to put him on a horse
with side-reins and let him ride without reins.
Once he has balance, there should be no reason
for him to stiffen the arms. With a majority of
riders one sees them almost 'beating time' with
their hands as the horse's action throws them

about. The arms should not be allowed to wave about: the rider should make, as it were, a counter movement to steady them even if the upper body is still being affected. In fact they should be so quiet that the horse does not suffer being jabbed in the mouth with each stride and indeed so steady that a glass of water held while trotting is not spilled. This is not a joke: every rider should try this out some time.

Obviously to keep the hands steady while the body is being thrown about demands that the rider is in positive control of his hands. The best way to do this deliberately is to give them something to do. Consciously telling oneself that one has to keep the hands steady is counter-productive and they revert to being stiff. It is a good idea to take a whip or stick in each hand, holding them vertically. It is then easy to see by any movement how steady the hands are. In this way, control of the hands can be developed and the awareness of the hands increases. The rider should continue this method of holding a whip or stick at all stages in his career as an occasional check on the steadiness of his hands. It is indeed rare to see a horseman with really quiet hands.

The hands should not be thought of as belonging in a fixed place. Normally, unless some special movement is required, they rest close together in front of the body (see illustration 21), their height and distance from the body being such as will allow them, at any time, to give, or go forward, without the rider being forced to alter his seat.

Forearms and upper arms form approximately a right-angle so that, by extending the arms, one can give with the reins. The upper arms hang down loosely. They should neither be stretched wide nor pressed against the body. Neither should the elbows be in contact with the body, as this would encourage a stiff, forced position. The height of the hands is contingent on the position of the horse's mouth: the reins and rider's forearm should, when viewed from the side, form a straight line. The rider's hips should try to maintain contact with his forearms: this gives one what is called a compact seat. In

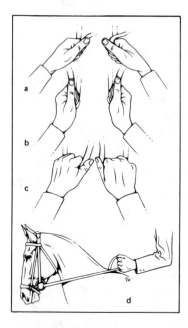

21 Holding the reins:

a: Correct; the hands are upright with the backs of the hands making a straight line with the forearms.

b: Wrong; wrists are bent, which makes for stiffness.

c: Wrong; hands are turned down so that they cannot be used sensitively and will lead the rider to make use of his arms.

d: Correct; forearm and upper arm make a right-angle with the reins, backs of the hands and forearms making a straight line.

achieving this compactness, however, one should not bring the arms back towards the body, but, on the contrary, bring the body towards the arms. This is because of the need to keep the horse forward onto the bit, and the driving force that is necessary for this tends to make the body go forward against the forearms.

Any attempt to influence with the reins can only be made sensitively if a soft contact has been established between hands and horse's mouth. A slack rein means that swift movement with it will inevitably have the effect of jerking the horse in the mouth. Before any rein influence can be given, it is essential that the horse be ready to obey such an aid: in other words, ridden forward onto the bit. Consequently one acts first with back and legs and then with the reins (see the section 'Making a horse obedient to the aids' on p. 69).

Rein influences are as follows:

1   Giving with both reins or just with one: for this one turns the hands appropriately or allows both hands and arms to go forward.

2   Taking back both reins or just one: here the rein is shortened by twisting or screwing the fists, such a shortening to be measured in millimetres or not more than a centimetre. But one should never move the whole arm and initiate a tugging match, for the horse is much stronger and will always win such a contest.

3   A passive maintaining of the rein tension on both sides or on one only in which the fists remain still.

If one were to attempt to give rein influences totally on their own, it would be found that:

1   The reins would hang slack when the rider gave: this must not occur and it happens because the driving influences are not present.

2   Taking back the reins becomes a tug at the reins: this is equally to be avoided and, once again, the absence of driving influences is the reason.

3   Nothing happens when the rider maintains passive rein pressure. It is the keeping of a

steady rein pressure while driving with back and legs that is the most important and the most difficult.

Rein control may only be learned on a horse, then, when one simultaneously pays attention to reins, back and legs.

a One should learn to give rein influences on both sides, i.e. giving, taking back and maintaining equal contact with both reins in the walk on, in trot and when halting. (See 'Lessons' p. 114. The most searching test of the main error – pulling at the reins – is to be found in the lesson 'The rein-back', p. 118 *et seq.*)

b The best way to learn rein influencing on one side, left or right (taking back with the one rein and keeping the other in position and then the other way round) is at turns at the halt, both on the forehand and on the quarters. Such lessons, particularly those on the quarters, are of inestimable value to the rider in showing him how the various influences dovetail together and how their correct use influences the horse.

Using one rein or employing differing weights of rein are required when one rides with collection, in turns and in the canter. However, if a rider wants to make correct use of this in forward movements, he must fully understand what influences it has on the horse at the halt.

The movement of the hands to be effective will vary with the kind of bridle and the way the reins are held. If one uses a bridle with a curb bit, double reins (with two reins in each hand – 2:2) are the easiest to use. The reins should be held in such a way that the gentler snaffle bit comes into action first and the stronger curb bit subsequently. This rein usage has the advantage that, when the horse changes its direction, the rider does not need to re-arrange the reins in order to avoid the outside curb rein from acting (see 'Turns in motion', p. 130). This method is the one to use when hacking out and jumping, for, as the degree of extension increases, the rider can give with both hands along the horse's neck without losing the reins.

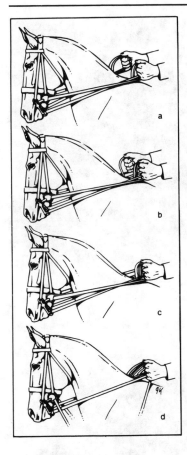

22 The most common methods of holding reins with a curb bit:

a: Divided reins; a suitable way for beginners to hold the reins, it is necessary for jumping or going across difficult terrain, but is far too often used to make a horse bend or flex.

b: With the snaffle bit acting: basic military method of rein-holding; the left hand is exactly in front of the middle of the body and the right hand close to it and in front of the right hip. The left hand holds three reins and the right hand one and this is therefore called 3:1.

c: Reins held in one hand only and in front of the body; also known as 'straight through' snaffle.

d: Simple snaffle grip: this demands a responsive horse, one which 'carries' itself, and a sensitive hand in the rider.

Something that is totally to be condemned – and one sees it often – is a rider using the strongly acting curb rein with force to bring his horse to a halt.

Holding the reins 3:1 requires much longer training and more practice. As the left hand should be in front of the body centrally and the right hand in front of the right hip, the arrangement is an unsymmetrical one. If both hands are held in front of the body, the curb acts crookedly. This is a sure way to bring about bad riding. The advantage of holding the reins 3:1 is that refined degrees of rein influences may be given because the rider is obliged to exercise control mainly with the left hand. The left hand is usually the weaker one, and riders using one hand only tend to expend less effort, which leads to greater sensitivity. In fact, taking the reins in just one hand means less expenditure of effort.

A person used to a 3:1 rein arrangement will find difficulties with the Fillis method, since the snaffle and curb reins are held differently and the fists must be used in a different way. Any turning of the wrist that raises the little finger upward towards the chest acts strongly on the curb rein which is positioned underneath. A rider should therefore try to dispense with this action if he possibly can. If he is used to holding the reins in other ways, he may well find this impossible and this method of rein control will prove to be too powerful.

The current trend in dressage tests is for a majority to adopt divided reins (2:2). When beginners commence riding instruction they should start with a snaffle and only move on to curb reins when some skill has been acquired.

a Learning initially with a snaffle is easier because the reins are easier to hold and therefore more readily understood.

b Riding with curb reins is better in that horses go well with them (as if side-reins were being used) and there is less movement.

The most difficult thing to learn with regard to rein use is that influences should be given with minimum pressure and not in isolation. Influen-

23 Snaffle bridle with dropped noseband.

24 Snaffle bridle with flash noseband.

25 Snaffle bridle with cavesson noseband.

26 Double bridle.

ces with the back, legs and body should take precedence, since all movement should stem from forward-impelling influences just as an aeroplane is impelled by engine and propellor.

A curb can be more painful for a horse because its action is that of a lever. It is essential, then, to ride young horses, to reschool badly-schooled ones and to teach horses to obey the aids, with the simple snaffle. If desired, one can, when riding a horse used to a curb, dispense with the curb action by allowing the curb rein to go slack. This should also be done in the case of the horse bucking, shying, refusing a jump and so on. A horse accepts a snaffle more readily because it is kinder but a curb is indispensable in perfecting dressage work. Rein use, just like leg activity, must become a reflex action for all riders to the extent that they do not need to think about it.

The movements which the hands make to control the reins should at all times be no more than a slight turning: riding instructors tend to talk far too much about this, and every aid, even that for turning, should stem from the seat. Every turn of the wrist, whether to yield with a rein or to influence, is slight and easy to practise. It is incorrect to try to give an aid for turning using rein alone, or more or less alone. That is simply being a coachman. And it is so very incorrect that we shall not attempt to describe the hand movement, the more to emphasise its small extent.

Clearly it is of no value for the beginner to practise rein influence while seated on an inanimate object; and it would teach him bad habits, for he would tend to use the hands without the accompanying influences of back and legs. Even if it is stressed to him that the accompaniment is vital he would be learning the lesson in an intellectual sense only without there being practical confirmation. Trial and practice are invariably of more lasting value than mere instruction.

INFLUENCES USING THE BACK

A rider can only influence with his back if the legs are used simultaneously: as we remarked, he can cause a tilting of a stool only if his feet are on the ground. If, while seated on the stool, he raises his legs, and if, while riding a horse he takes his legs away from the saddle, he will not be able to exert any influence. The way the muscles are used in back-bracing is discussed on page 23. It is by no means difficult to explain the action but it is not easy to convey its significance and correct use.

Back-muscle influence is at the very heart of all riding theory. The back is, at all times, the connection between legs and reins, and the influences stemming from legs and reins can work together if a simultaneous action of the back unites them closely. The back gives the downbeat, as it were; almost the command 'Act now!' None of the influences must come in late or be absent, otherwise the aid will simply not make sense to the horse. It is therefore just not possible for a rider to try out influencing with the back in isolation.

If a rider on a well-schooled horse with his legs in contact with the horse braces his back while giving with the reins, he will find that the horse moves on. If his reins remain steady, the horse will give him halt.

That the effects are different is clearly nothing to do with the back but is caused solely by the rein action. The back action was the same in both cases. Should the rider be on a less well-schooled horse, he will find leg pressure is necessary but this must be applied at exactly the same time as the back-bracing and hand action. If a rider asks for walk on or halt without this back use, he will only succeed by exerting stronger leg pressure to obtain walk on, and stronger rein pressure to obtain halt: in other words his aids become much rougher. The more sensitive a horse, the more it dislikes rough aids, and nervous and timid horses, and particularly thoroughbreds, will readily refuse or 'go on strike'.

The more advanced and refined the quality of riding, the greater the significance of back influencing. In correcting faults in badly schooled horses, particularly those with bad backs, the mastering of back influence is of massive importance. Many horses seem unrideable because their rider is not capable of exerting this back influence.

We maintain this because the rider must be able to harmonise his back, legs and reins: we do not talk of rein aids or leg aids but designate

27 The back muscles relaxed at a
working trot. Felix Bürkner riding
Bober.

28 Bracing the back in the transition
to medium trot. The 'compact' seat.
Adjutant Patrick Le Rolland (France)
on Cramique, in Aachen, 1973.

29 The back braced strongly when asking for halt from a medium trot. Felix Bürkner riding Rosenkelch.

such activities as influencing with reins or legs, with the aids owing their existence to the mutually interacting influences. And this is why we refuse to countenance the notion of practising rein influences in isolation, so important is it to learn the importance of the influences acting together.

An aid is comprehended by the horse as an aid and it will be fully effective only if horse and rider are working in total sympathy and unity. This will seem self-evident but it needs emphasising because, invariably, when a rider gives an aid, he and the horse will be moving actively at the vital moment and the rider will tend to lose bodily contact. It is absolutely essential that, for the aid to be given completely effectively, at the split second when the aid is given, man and horse are in perfect coordination, in other words, the rider is sitting deeply and evenly in the saddle.[1]

[1]After all, the perfect dining-car waiter must learn to serve clients in a swaying environment. If he cannot acquire the art of balance and an ability to follow the swayings of the carriage, he will perform the 'hot gravy trick' over the laps of the diners. And if a bus starts unexpectedly, the unwary passenger will stagger backwards and would find it very difficult to light a cigar at that precise moment.

Should the rider, at the moment of giving the aids, find himself behind the movement, it is out of the question that they can be harmonious and effective and each influence that he tries to exert will be accompanied by varying tuggings and jerkings. Harmony, sitting deeply in the saddle and going with the horse in all its movements can only be achieved by bracing the back.

Every horseman who has not yet learned to influence with his back or who, despite the long-standing evidence, is not convinced of its efficacy, should try out the exercises described on page 26 on a really well-schooled horse: that is the way he will improve his feel and his influence.

When riding with collection, at all turns and at the canter it is essential that the rider push forward his inside seat-bone and hip. That is a simple statement but the rider who does not comprehend what his instructor is after by his command 'Hip forward!', because he has not practised it, will achieve nothing more than a stiffening of his body. (A description of these exercises was given on page 27.) If the rider uses his back muscles on one side only, in other words pushes forward just one seat-bone and the corresponding hip, then, if a condition of harmony is in being between rider and horse, the addition of a slight displacement of weight will suffice to make the horse go collectedly, turn, canter on and execute flying changes.

It is important and necessary that a rider learns from the very beginning to influence with his back to avoid the habit of giving ineffective aids: early bad habits are difficult to eradicate. Every child knows how to use his back when on a swing and therefore why should not every rider be able to use a method of influence that he once possessed? He will then in his very first lessons have an idea of how to sit properly and will know what his instructor requires in asking that his seat be pushed rather more forward in the saddle: 'You must wipe the saddle from back to front with your seat!' (A strange figure of speech!) 'Body backward! Chest forward!' These are not the ways in which an instructor should seek to correct faults, for he is not getting at the root cause. 'Imagine you wanted to lean back as if the saddle were fitted with a chair-back!' This will not do. A rider should certainly not sit leaning forward, but this will be corrected only by *bracing the back* and not by a series of commands such as 'Body backward! Chest forward!' They will serve only to make him go stiff.

Schooling the horse

Every rider who schools his horse must do his mental homework in addition to the practical work before he will understand it. He will need to take account of the horse's conformation, its movements, its capacity for work, its character and its temperament. He should lose no opportunity of seeking the knowledge of more experienced riders and, by watching other riders and horses, improve his own judgement. He should try to ride unfamiliar horses, for each horse differs in physique and temperament and so gives a rider fresh points to deal with and widens his practical experience. The horse is invariably the best instructor and the more horses one can ride, the more feeling one can amass for that required harmony between rider and horse.

But a note of warning should be sounded at this stage: every rider who undertakes to school a horse should do so in a humane manner and with compassion in order that the teaching be carried out correctly. He must be patient in all contingencies and not deal out over-hasty, unjustified punishment. 'Boys will be boys', so if a young horse acts in the spirit of this adage it must be treated with tolerance or one will turn it into something worse than a dead machine. One can replace worn-out parts in a dead machine but damage to tendons and joints, to the nerves and spirit of a horse can never be made good.

A horse usually attains full size at three years old,[1] when its joints and muscles and tendons are strong enough for its own weight. But problems arise if it then has to bear the additional weight of a rider, although most horses manage to cope

[1]Geldings grow until they are six years old.

with this. The rider may then be tempted – especially with a willing horse – to start lessons which the horse will almost certainly carry out badly since its body is not yet adequately developed.

The average horse will make many thousands of jumps in its career. Each time it has to land on its legs. To jump a young horse too soon, and especially over high jumps, adds many more such landings. One knows of far too many young horses ruined in this way for the rest of their lives. One sees six and seven-year-olds who look tired out. And this is before the age at which they should reach their peak: their legs are tired and they just do not want to jump. These are truly sad creatures, the ones who are victims in their adolescence to man's unthinking vanity and selfishness!

The true cavalier – and that is what we should all try to be – feels responsible for the sensitive animal and, in schooling his horse, tries to create a positive working schedule: he attempts, by appropriate dressage work, to provide a solid platform on which he can systematically build. He will always ensure that his horse is working willingly and avoids asking too much of it. If a horse is worked with these points in mind, muscles, tendons and joints will be strengthened and the horse will grow confident. And then, when the horse is totally ready in both physical and mental respects, just as ripe fruit falls from the tree, more demanding lessons and higher jumps come naturally.

A horse schooled with this care will be a pleasure to its rider for many years to come.

CHAPTER TWO
Schooling the Horse

The nature of the horse

The horse is very good-natured and trusting and much more sensitive than is generally realised. It is very fond of being caressed, has an excellent memory and an amazingly well-developed sense of direction and locality. It is quick to acquire habits and retains them firmly. But it is much less bright and harder to teach than a dog, is timid and easily frightened by harsh treatment and punishment.

It is essential, then, that the rider be capable of understanding and evaluating all these characteristics, which, of course, vary from horse to horse. It is supremely important for one to turn to good account the horse's qualities of docility and memory and persistence in habits. And it must never be lost sight of that it is a sensitive creature and a living being with its own psychology and not to be used as if it were a piece of machinery.

Every difficulty that one encounters in riding has a specific cause: unfortunately, apparently similar difficulties may have different causes. If he does not take account of this fact – and recognising the causes is the hard part – a rider will never be able to rectify faults. A horse is easily frightened and much more anxious than man. Fear is most commonly the reason for shying, stopping, jumping sideways, kicking, rearing and also for the less obvious signs of unhappiness such as uneven steps, head-tossing, tail-waving, tensing certain muscles and hollowing the back. It is important that, like a good schoolteacher, one should take account of both the horse's temperament and his restricted intelligence and not attribute difficulties to a deliberate stubbornness ('He just won't'), and search for the cause in one's own actions. One will do best with consideration and calmness, never with impatience and punishment that the horse usually does not understand and cannot understand and which will end by making him even more fearful.

Riding demands of the practitioner that he, at all times, thinks himself into the very mind of his horse. Only when he thinks as the horse thinks can he understand whether the aids and influences which he wishes to impart have been grasped. In this connection one must not lose sight of the horse's herd instinct which leads, as a matter of nature, to problems and so-called bad habits. The horse has a natural tendency to do what other horses do and therefore tries to stay with them. This is something a rider has to bear in mind. Indeed this herd instinct can be turned to good account in schooling. A horse will jump an obstacle more willingly if it sees other horses at the far side and, again, will make a jump more willingly if given a 'lead' by another horse. In the hunting field horses jump freely one after the other. Timid horses will go past objects that frighten them far more readily when in company: for example, a horse may shy when asked to pass a lorry or similar piece of machinery, but can accustom itself to these objects if given a lead by another horse. A thinking rider takes advantage of this company and then tries again on his own, while the lead horse waits patiently. Such care is psychologically necessary and desirable, for it would be totally wrong for a rider to want to impose his will on his horse, regardless of the latter's fears. He would accomplish that only by harsh aids that the horse would fear more than the object that first frightened it. No purpose would be served save that of instilling fears in the horse and outraging the most elementary principles of psychology and training. The horse would never lose its timidity: rather it would be found that from some distance away it begins to worry at a possibly frightening object, thinking of the punishment it expects to receive there so it tries to turn aside or even to run back the way it has come.

The horse has a remarkable memory, especially for pain that it may have suffered in the past. It will never in its whole life forget, say, being struck by a vehicle or colliding with a wall in a school. It requires a sensitive and patient teacher in such cases to restore the animal's sense of confidence.

Account should also be taken of the fact that to wait around near the door of the school will give a horse a tendency to stop when in that vicinity and try to make a crafty way back to its stable. A similar danger exists in the lazy habit that riders have when returning from a hack when they give away the reins on nearing home, allowing the horse to make its own way back to the stable. A horse soon gets used to the idea, and, on a different occasion when its rider picks up the reins in order to ride away from home again, objects to going in the required direction. It is not the horse's bad habit that should be held to blame for this but the rider's lack of perception of how his horse's mind works.

The aim of schooling

The aim of schooling a horse is that a rider should be able to do all that he wants to do with his horse with the minimum of exertion on his part and the greatest possible consideration for the horse. The training that brings this about is dressage, and this means building up the horse's physique to its maximum capability and teaching it obedience.

It is very simple to state the purpose of dressage and the statement sounds as if it should have a general application, but, in practice, riders have very different aims in mind and they have very different ideas as to what they hope to achieve with their horses. This multiplicity of aims cannot be fulfilled by the same method, which means that there cannot be one single training schedule. Very often, though, schedules which appear dissimilar are, on reflection, based on similar foundations and they complement rather than contradict each other. This requires elaboration, since problems, doubts and mistakes often manifest themselves if the practitioner does not keep his goal firmly in mind.

a *A dressage rider* who intends to succeed at the highest level in dressage events requires a well-made horse of quality, with a noble bearing and with outstanding natural action. Strength, stamina and jumping ability are of secondary importance. Initially in dressage tests the novice horse will be judged on appearance[1] and aptitude and, as the training becomes more complex, go on to more advanced dressage tests.

b *The show-jumper* obviously needs a horse with the best jumping talent. He can take less account of elegance and above-average action and ignore small faults in conformation. Good performances will be achieved only by horses with a natural talent for jumping and whose aptitude has been fully developed by special training. But such horses must be obedient to be able to comply with the rider's guiding in the tight turns of a jumping course and, for this, it is essential that they obey the aids. This last point is often neglected.

c *The 'general purpose' rider* chooses a horse that has a good deal of the qualities that make up both dressage and jumping horses. It is important that it should have a good gallop, strength and stamina. The goal here is *'eventing'*, which is also one of the disciplines in the Olympic Games.

d *The casual rider* contents himself with being able to ride in comfort at all paces. His horse should be easy to turn and bring to a halt and should canter well. His type of horse should therefore be very obedient, but not necessarily capable of great performance and endurance. Riders in this category usually want to present a good appearance and, if the horse is to carry itself well, it needs to be well schooled.

---

[1] By 'appearance' is implied the judging simply of the way the horse looks without taking into account the progress of its schooling. However, in addition to build and temperament, the way a horse goes is taken into account and a well-ridden dressage horse makes a much better impression than a raw or carelessly presented one.

e *The rider to hounds* must have a horse that can gallop, jump well and have endurance. It must be keen enough to go on without needing to be pushed constantly, but – and this is most important – not rush to the front too impetuously. In this aspect of riding, it may be said that the horse's innate qualities and training are more important than careful dressage. Appearance and elegance are of less value here.

f *The race rider* simply requires the fastest possible horse. In this connection, dressage would be more or less superfluous. Speed is a corollary of a racehorse's breeding and simple training will bring it to perfection.

g *The circus rider* seeks to offer an uninformed public a similar spectacle to that which a dressage rider exhibits. But the profit motive is more significant than the attainment of a harmony between himself and his horse (although he is very keen to have this). His intention is to dazzle his uneducated audience with brilliant trick movements and paces, and, as his horse will not need to be ridden out across country, special schooling will accomplish this more quickly than the time it would take to make a dressage horse by comprehensive training.

The aims discussed above prescribe the varying ways in which a horse may be schooled. Often, in each category, riders will stop short of reaching an ideal state of achievement in the interests of saving themselves time and work.

All the horses that are intended for participation in dressage tests, jumping tests and eventing, as well as those marked out for hunting or just hacking, need to have dressage training after they have learned their basics and this will be described in the following sections. Following that, their further schooling will take a specialised turn depending on what the rider has in mind for them.

If time and good instructors permit, systematic dressage can bring nothing but benefit to any horse and pleasure to the rider. If, however, the dressage is misapplied, is carried out in an

30 Maximum extension over a jump. Nelson Pessoa on Gran Geste.

31 Extreme collection in the levade.

over-hasty manner and in an insensitive way – and this is more often than not the case – then more harm is done than good. What is difficult is to recognise whether dressage is being well applied or badly. The old saying is valid in this connection: 'As ye sow, so ye shall reap!'

Basic views on dressage

It is generally assumed that attitudes on schooling will have changed greatly in the course of centuries and from country to country. One speaks of the classical art of riding, of the German and the Roman schools.

The classical art of riding is not a set of fixed precepts, any more than Baroque or Renaissance styles are defined by particular ornamentation or architectural guidelines. It must be looked at as a complete entity representing all objectives and the paths to these objectives in the art of riding. The classical art of riding might best be defined as the method of training that seeks to establish the most complete rapport between rider and horse in the most natural way possible and with the utmost consideration for the horse. It rejects totally everything that contradicts nature, artificiality and artificial paces.

Both the German and Roman schools have a similar concept. They are closely related to each other. Their differences have been shaped by the differences of temperament and character of the countries involved. The German is more thorough and academic while the Frenchman more delicate, with a strong feeling for elegance. In England and Italy dressage used to be considered of lesser importance.

There are always differences of opinion in every field. Just as lawyers and doctors who are considered eminent in their fields often form different judgements from each other, so do riding authorities, and, after all, it must be borne in mind that riding is not like mathematics which deals in fixed and immutable measurements and quantities, but is concerned with feeling, temperament and capability of horse, rider and instructor: in other words, with qualities that are not absolute. The difficulty in arriving at unanimity is due, more often than not, to the fact that those who hold the conflicting opinions cannot even agree on a starting point and that definitions, catchphrases and technical expressions are used which may have definite meanings but tend to be understood and interpreted in different ways. Nevertheless, since Xenophon, writer of the earliest known riding manual, it has been agreed that the procedure to be followed in dressage is dictated by the degree of ambition of the practitioner, by the time available for practice, by the quality of the horse and by the ability, disposition and temperament of the rider.

The procedure in schooling

One may divide up normal schooling into three different stages:

Stage one:
the totally untrained horse is taught to accept a rider on its back.

Stage two:
the horse is taught the aids.

Stage three:
when the horse has learned these, it is (a) taught to obey, and (b) its real training begins.

Stage one is obligatory for every horse that is to be ridden in any capacity. Similarly, stage two is obligatory for almost every horse. A horse needs to understand thoroughly what the aids mean before it can be expected to carry them out. Once a horse has learned to obey the aids cleanly and quickly, it is ready for any demand. One finds, all too often, that the horse has not been taught this proper understanding. Stage three is the real training of the horse, the dressage stage. If the horse is destined for a special role, this stage may be replaced by an appropriate specialised training. The conclusion of stage two is therefore the parting of the ways of the steps in training.

Stage one in training

THE TOTALLY UNTRAINED HORSE IS TAUGHT TO ACCEPT A RIDER ON ITS BACK

A horse that has never carried a rider can only find the weight of a person more or less of a discomfort on its back. Its natural timidity will make it apprehensive about the whole business and its fear will be the greater if the rider is clumsy in his actions. On the very first occasion of putting the saddle in place, one should pat the horse and speak gently to it. The words, needless to say, are unimportant: it is the tone of voice that matters. But every ill-considered step and every fault committed will affect vitally the horse's attitude, such is its retentive memory and apprehensiveness. It should therefore be saddled and bridled in the environment it knows best – in its stall or box – and by its own rider while the groom pats the horse's neck.

It is often useful if the horse is then lunged (see p. 189), particularly if its back muscles tense up or if it takes shortened, anxious steps on being led out of its stall. If the horse shows such signs, it would be wrong to get on its back immediately. And, if, when it has been backed, it still shows these tensions, it is advisable to cure them by lungeing. The more considerately and slowly one works initially, the more rapid and confident will be the subsequent progress and the fewer the reversals. Each time one mounts the young horse, it is advisable to proceed almost as if from the beginning and enlist the aid of the person who looks after the horse or someone else. This person should be instructed to pat the horse's neck and speak soothingly to it and lead it forward immediately the rider is seated. Hasty movements upset the horse.

Horses with an equable disposition will respond to the skilled rider by accepting the burden and adjust their balance suitably. The rider must, however, sit still, not attempt to use influences in any way and use the whip to urge the horse forward into a gentle trot. In this way one will minimise and banish all the horse's tensions that arise from having to carry a rider in equilibrium and from the muscle-tensions stemming from fear.

It is an advantage if the young horse can go accompanied by an older lead horse: it will soon learn reassurance from the latter's calmness.

For the first few times it is recommended that the rider walk on as soon as he has mounted, for the horse is more incommoded by its load when immobile, and hence its tensions will be reduced on walking forward.

Once the horse has learned to accept the rider's weight, it will move naturally again, having tended to take uncertain, short and clumsy steps when first mounted. Calm, even and long strides will indicate when the rider is succeeding. But any attempt to influence with the hands will make things difficult. One should also avoid tiring the horse by trotting for too long a period or indeed prolonging the lesson unduly. If the horse beings to feel a sense of strain, it will get excited. In between trotting periods it will be found that treating the horse with affection, stroking and patting its neck and speaking to it soothingly, will be far more effective than any aid. Most effective of all is a calm seat. The rider must avoid relinquishing a good position in the saddle to lean forward in the mistaken belief that he will take the strain off the horse's quarters. If the horse then does anything untoward, his position in the saddle will vary, he will lurch forward and cause far more disturbance than if he sat quietly with braced back, going with the movement. Absolutely the best way for the rider to make life easy and pleasant for his horse is for him to sit in a supple manner. But if he leans backward and if he sits rigidly and stiffly in the saddle, he will not be in a position to brace his back and go with the movement. Such a rider should not undertake the schooling of a young horse.

Stage two in training

MAKING A HORSE OBEDIENT TO THE AIDS

This stage in a horse's training is so vital and yet so frequently misunderstood that it needs thorough explanation. It will be given this in the light of the following points:

How does a horse appear when obeying the aids?

How does a rider know when his horse is obeying the aids?

How is this achieved?

How does one reschool a horse if this obedience has been lost?

What do we mean by 'making a horse obedient to the aids'?

A horse is obeying the aids completely if:

1   It is totally relaxed. There must be no tension or stiffness at all in jaw-bones, poll, lower jaw, neck, back or legs. This applies to joints and muscles.

2   It is attentive to the rider's legs, back, reins and moves in equilibrium. This means in effect that the complete moving mechanism of the horse is willingly subjected to its rider's commands. This is only possible if the horse understands the influences of legs, hands, weight and back and will willingly carry out what those components say to it.

Teaching a horse the aids does not mean:

a   that it has to adopt a particular position or carriage, or

b   that it already understands all the aids that are made up by the various influences.

The horse should – completely relaxed – be capable of carrying out small demands made on it by its rider (see pp. 75 *et seq.*) and give him a feeling of harmony or oneness at both trot and canter. It will require a much longer period of time before this feeling is achieved fully at the walk and at halt. A foundation is gradually established on which the training can be developed. It is almost impossible for a proper working relationship to exist between rider and horse unless the latter trusts the former completely and is totally relaxed. If only one of the ideals mentioned in points (1) and (2) above is missing, then a whole host of difficulties will ensue which, depending on the horse's temperament and the skill of the rider, may lead to a complete breakdown in schooling and will at the least mean that the rider will not succeed in carrying out his intentions.

Running through the aids is, then, the starting point for all dressage work and is absolutely essential to it. It is just as necessary in other disciplines that a rider has in mind for his horse, for example in jumping. Applying the aids and making the horse obey them should be the start of any lesson, no matter whether it be a simple or a difficult one. It must be remembered, however, that the rider must first have the attention of his horse and that it be relaxed and willing, and then he can expect that it will carry out his instructions.

Applying the aids is also something the rider must go back to if his horse shows any kind of disobedience, tenseness or similar problems. Any ruined or badly schooled horse that has lost its good paces or becomes apprehensive must first be made attentive to the aids. Once this is successful, the difficulties and tensions disappear, the paces are restored and, in short, the essential harmony between rider and horse will be reaffirmed.

Maintaining and refining this harmony to a degree of perfection in even the most difficult lessons is the touchstone for judging whether the schooling is being carried out on the right lines. Every brick that is added to the edifice of dressage serves to refine this harmony; if it does not, it will lead to an aberration. That is a simple statement but it is the most difficult fact in all riding and quite the most important because the most indispensable.

It must be said that most horses have not been taught the aids, or have been taught them only incompletely, and such horses, when ridden out, can be controlled and directed without perfect harmony to some extent. But it is beyond dispute that the same horses, when fully obedient to the aids, will go with less expenditure of energy and much more happily and that the rider will control them calmly and with less effort, will feel more in control of the situation, will enjoy himself and will not experience unexpected problems. But his horse must be obedient to the aids!

What does a horse look like when obeying the aids?
We ask this question because it is often posed in this form. One should not try to answer it by describing a horse carrying itself in a way that suggests perfection. If one were to do that, one

would be inciting a majority of riders to force their horses into that ideal form, something that is most dangerous for any rider. One will not then look to observe how a horse carries itself. The carriage or appearance of a horse will vary according to the degree of schooling attained, to the pace, to what is being attempted and to the conformation of the animal. The correct answer to the question posed above can only be: 'As if there is perfect harmony between rider and horse.'

And it is not possible to answer the question: 'How does a horse look when obeying the aids?', for one cannot talk of the horse totally in isolation, since the whole aspect of the horse's obeying the aids is inextricably bound up with the rider who has to give them.

However, it does happen that people speak of the way a horse carries itself, and, if they have to do that, they should not limit themselves to neck and head: it cannot be over-emphasised that a rider has a living being under him – not a wooden horse. With a wooden horse it may be possible to work one component in isolation, but that is impossible with a real horse and it is wrong to judge the whole by one or some of the parts.

The requirement that harmony between rider and horse should be recognisable suggests that something more than a quick glance is necessary for judgement: both rider *and* horse should be studied for some time before one can say whether or not the horse is obeying the aids. And it is essential that they be observed at the halt and in motion, in changing the lead, turning corners, in coming to a halt and in circling. It is perfectly possible for a horse to obey the aids at an ordinary trot but not at the halt. Should it, however, appear that the reverse applies, i.e that the horse seems to be attentive to the aids at halt but not when going forward, then one has most certainly judged wrongly.

Every movement must be made calmly and with harmony and must appear so. The movements that the rider makes must be correct in themselves and be in harmony with the horse.

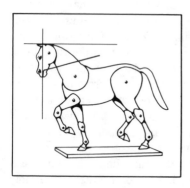

32 A wooden puppet-horse.

The horse should look to an observer as if it is at ease and the rider should give the appearance that he is sitting doing nothing, with everything happening by itself as a matter of course. It is of paramount importance that the aids should be invisible. If they can be seen, they are not in harmony, and the logical deduction is that the horse has not been taught the aids.

> No illustration of a horse listening to the aids is given in order to avoid a wrong emphasis on external appearance.
>
> HARMONY
> between
> RIDER AND HORSE
>
> does not exist at an odd moment in time as might be caught by an isolated sketch. It is best expressed, not by the horse having a special carriage, but by the complete and constant accord of *two* living bodies in every movement.

33 How a horse looks which is listening to the aids.

1 The rider[1] must:

    a sit, at all times, calmly and with suppleness in the deepest part of the saddle. He must not lurch about in the saddle at every stride, nor should an onlooker hear or see him slapping back into the saddle;

    b keep arms and hands still. He must not work his hands and arms at every stride. His rein contact must be constant. The reins must not hang slackly, or be slack at one moment and strongly applied the next. Nor must the rider saw with the reins to keep contact with the horse's mouth or to keep the horse mouthing the bit;

    c keep his legs still and in constant contact with the horse: they can thus influence if required without the rider changing his position. It is permissible to

[1] Judging can start with horse or rider: we shall start with the rider because he is the active component in asking for the aids.

make a slight movement of the knee, which may need to be bent or straightened ever so slightly.

2 The horse must:

a take calm, even, but energetic steps;

b when going forward, be perfectly straight with both ears at the same height; at corners and when turning it must give the appearance of bending of its own volition towards the inside. Stiffness will manifest itself if the horse's head is turned to the outside;

c mouth the bit calmly and steadily all the time without it being audible. It must not try to spit the bit out, grind it or play with it with its tongue. It should not get its tongue over the bit, let it hang out or make foam;

d keep head and neck still. It should not shake its head, even at a change of pace or a halt or when trotting on from rest, nor stretch it forward or upward or lower it to its chest. The neck should form an even, curved line;

e carry the tail quietly with no twitching or swishing.

It is self-apparent that all the above requirements must be present in equal measure. If just one of them is absent, the horse will not be in a state of total relaxation, nor be able to put its mechanism fully at the disposal of its rider. It will not be in a position to respond to the aids.

Similarly, the rounded neck and constant mouthing of the bit are not the only features, nor the most important ones, but are merely the easiest ones to observe. But horses can round their necks and mouth the bit without their being in a position to obey the aids.

HOW CAN A RIDER TELL IF HIS HORSE IS OBEYING THE AIDS?

This question is, of necessity, much more important for the rider than the point dealt with in the previous section, 'What does it look like?'

One must be very clear as to what the rider

should feel and how he can verify that he has interpreted this correctly.

Every rider should accept that there are definite tests for judging whether or not his horse is obeying the aids.

A horse listening to the aids is:

1 completely relaxed
2 listening to the rider's legs and back
3 aware of and ready to obey the reins
4 balanced.

Each of these four requirements needs to be dealt with separately. But it should not be assumed that they can be achieved independently of each other. They all merge into one another, for the aids are a combination of back, leg, rein and weight influences which are inseparable. One cannot use the reins without the legs or the legs without the reins. One can only make a horse ready to obey the aids.

How a rider can tell if his horse is totally relaxed
This point is such an all-embracing one that an answer will only be possible in the light of checking and testing what is treated in the next chapters. If there is any hint of resistance, the horse is not completely relaxed. This is particularly so when the horse:

a does not go forward evenly, with a long stride and mouthing the bit, or
b if the swing of its back is uneven, so that its rider cannot sit deeply in the saddle.

How a rider can tell if his horse is obeying his legs and back
The tests of whether a horse is listening to legs and back are so closely related to each other that it is almost impossible to separate them: influencing with the back is not possible without the support of the legs and the influence that these give can be delivered so sensitively that it is often difficult to say whether the legs are simply in contact with the horse or whether they are being used actively. The rider himself, however, must always be aware of what he is doing.

A horse may be said to be obeying legs and back when, at any time and mainly by use of them, a rider can make it:

a go forward more actively
b take longer strides
c halt.

Additionally, a horse obeying the legs can, by their use, be made to:

d move over to the side.

The method of checking (a) and (d) does not need any special explanation. But it is more difficult to induce the horse to take longer strides. It will not do if the horse simply speeds up anxiously when legs and back are used with an appropriate yielding of the reins: it must not react adversely to these influences by raising and lowering its head, waving its head or tail, or similar objections. Its strides should continue to be calm and regular but lengthier. This must be practised before one can be sure of it. With a little practice, a rider will need only two or three such lengthened strides to know that his horse is responsive to back and legs. Without such practice, one will never know what one is looking for and the real danger then exists that the horse's good paces will be lost without its rider being aware of the fact.

It is just as difficult to make the opposite test, that of knowing whether the halt is *thorough*.[1] Many people maintain that for a halt to be thorough or complete, the horse should really listen more to the reins than to the back and legs. But this opinion reinforces most clearly the argument that one cannot make a division between the horse listening to the reins or listening to back and legs. One should always talk only of the horse 'obeying the aids'. And equally, if one is going to ask the horse to lengthen its stride, it must be regarded as part of the same requirement to ask the horse to halt, since it needs similar activity. For, after all, back and legs are

[1]'Thorough' means, in this connection, that the halt is successful if it affects the whole horse – mouth, neck, back and right down to the hind legs. On the other hand, one says that a halt 'breaks down' if the horse objects to pressure on its jaw with its jaw, poll or neck, by opening its mouth or shaking its head. In effect, then, the halt is not a complete one in that it does not affect the whole body back to the hind legs, and the horse lurches to a halt.

positive factors in both. If a horse is given forward-driving pressure with back and legs while the reins are kept steady or tightened, it should slow its pace and shorten its profile. Its action should become shorter and more elevated. But it should not show any evidence – raising or lowering its head, swinging head or tail, turning or throwing its neck, opening wide its mouth, or suchlike – that it regards being asked for halt as a discomfort.

For his part, the rider should get the feeling that the horse's hindquarters have become lower and its strides longer, even though the fact of the matter is that they have become slower. Sometimes, fresh horses, when asked to halt, will react to leg pressure with a small tail movement. If the movement is too great or if the horse shows in other ways that it finds the halt uncomfortable, then the halt was not a good one. It is possible to ask for a half-halt in a sensitive way or in a heavy-handed way. Most sensitive of all is when the rider does no more than brace his back. If he simultaneously applies equal leg pressure to push the horse forward, the action may still be considered as sensitive. But if the half-halt has to be accomplished more emphatically by a positive pulling of the reins, even if this is a small one, it must be regarded as coming into the category of heavy-handed. Often the rider will not know whether he has driven the horse forward into unyielding hands or brought about his effect by being active with the reins. Holding the reins in one hand only will make it easier to determine this.

If a horse is listening to the rider's back and legs, it will obey smaller influences they may impart. One can thus induce a horse to move its quarters to the inside by pushing forward the inside seat-bone accompanied by supporting outside leg pressure. If the horse reacts against the leg and moves its quarters in the opposite direction, then it is not leg-obedient. This asking his horse to move its quarters to left and right is a good test for the rider to establish whether or not his horse is responsive to his slightest leg pressure. It must do this before it can be said to be obeying the legs.

How a rider can tell if his horse is obeying the reins

A horse is obeying the reins when a rider can, at all times and mainly with the use of the reins, make his horse:

a carry its head higher or lower
b stretch its neck
c assume a flexed position
d relinquish a flexed position
e change its stance.

The horse is obeying the aids if the rider can carry out the above even with the reins held in one hand only. But this will not be possible without positive support from the back and legs. For this reason a careful observer will not seek to establish whether the horse is obeying the reins but that he is listening to the aids in all their ramifications.

1 If the rider raises or lowers his hands he can, within certain limits, raise or lower the horse's head. By using just one hand he can make the horse raise or lower one side of its head. The horse should respond immediately and willingly to such actions and, if it does not, it is not listening to the reins. The extent to which head-raising or lowering is possible will be marked by the horse's resistance or by the fact that the reins will go slack. Should a rider ask his horse to assume, for too long a period of time, a neck and head carriage that is more than its standard of training should call for, he will damage his cause. The position of neck and head should develop in a natural way: it should be found to be low when the horse is first acquainted with the aids, and then, with the horse's quarters becoming lower, its complete forward structure comes up, and its head position is raised.

2 If the rider gives with both reins while maintaining unchanged leg-pressure, the horse will have to stretch its neck forward, the amount depending on the degree of rein-yielding. Should the horse not extend its neck, the reins will hang slack and it may be

ment of the rider's weight. Displacing the weight forward or backward is very difficult to do without changing the position of the seat and this is detrimental to true feeling. But when the horse begins to obey back influence and can give a good halt, it is then said to be balanced. A horse must also accommodate itself to any lateral movement of the rider, whether to right or left, and bend or turn depending on the nature of the back, leg and rein influences. Furthermore, a rider should be able to give the reins away and yet ride a serpentine, but he will have to drive his horse well forward with back and legs.

When is a horse straight?
When viewed from above, all horses, in the natural order of things, are slightly bent. This is said to be bound up with the way the embryo lies in its mother's womb. In motion, this bend can be observed in the way that the hind legs do not quite follow the same line as the forelegs but will be to one side or the other by about a hand's width. Most horses (and this is also to be seen in dogs) go along with hind legs – through the body to the front legs – making a right-hand curve: in other words, the quarters are displaced slightly to the right. Such horses are less supple on the left side and, when riding them forward, the rider gets the feeling that the horse is leaning on the left rein and is not on the right rein.

It is necessary to work the horse with flexing to the left and circling to the left so that it will become more accommodating on the left side, will stretch itself to take up the right rein and the result will be that its hind legs follow the exact track of the forelegs. Horses with a natural bend in the other direction are, of course, worked the other way round.

A horse is said to be straight when it is equally flexible on both sides and the hind legs follow exactly the track made by the forelegs, no matter whether the horse is going in a straight line or circling. This is essential for all advanced training and for collection. Only a straight horse can go with proper equilibrium, with free, even paces and develop its natural swing (see illustration 4).

HOW IS A HORSE TAUGHT TO OBEY THE AIDS?

This question has to be answered in different ways, for a schooled horse, a totally unschooled horse and one that has been spoiled will all require a different method. The purposes and ultimate intentions are similar but it is necessary to discuss them one by one.

Something that one can achieve by a single aid with a schooled horse might take weeks of painstaking work with its unschooled counterpart and a similar period of time to correct faults in a horse that resists firmly its rider's intention. We therefore designate 'teaching a horse the aids' as a stage, and when a horse can pass this examination, so to speak, and obeys the aids, it has mastered this stage.

Making a schooled horse listen to the aids

If a rider wishes to make a schooled horse attentive to the aids, he has merely to brace his back. It is immaterial whether one is at halt, trotting or cantering – the horse will be listening to the aids, provided that a rein contact is maintained, i.e. no positive action is taken by the hands, and that the legs, which should always be in contact with the horse's body, can lend support to the back action by light pressure (see half-halt, pp. 115 *et seq.*).

A horse who does not immediately respond to back-muscle action and leg pressure has not been properly schooled. It must be regarded either as an unschooled or a spoiled horse.

Teaching an unschooled horse the aids

An unschooled horse may be taught the aids when it has progressed to the point when it is happy to carry the weight of a rider at a gentle trot with long, steady strides in the company of a lead horse. The time to begin the task is essentially when the horse seems to be bored and the rider has to urge it on, which should be done by a tap with the whip. This must be done with prudence, however, especially with a young horse, in order to avoid making it apprehensive or frightened. The rider then gradually puts his lower legs in closer contact with the horse, something that no horse will take exception to if the legs are quiet. Then, slight leg pressure reinforced by a tap with the whip will teach the horse that it is being required to go forward.

From this point, one works at making the horse go well forward at a working trot. This is a pace that is marginally quicker than the one the horse would choose. If the horse shows signs of shortening its strides and becoming generally lazier, it will lose its swing and impulsion. It then needs positive urging on and, when it is the rider who is dictating the pace and not simply letting his mount go at any pace it fancies, then the rider is being positive. This is the beginning of the horse's obedience to the aids. The swing in the pace must not be attempted by the rider trying to impose an outline on his horse with his hands. Impulsion will never be created by an enforced shape. All tensions and crookedness and all uneven strides must be ridden out forward, so to speak, with calm, lengthy paces in a working trot. As long as the rider does not become busy with his hands, the horse will lower its neck and head and will gradually, of its own accord, try to find an even support on the bit.

One should avoid changing the pace too early and too suddenly to a strong trot. Turns and changes of pace should only be hinted at in an exploratory manner. One feels one's way step by step and takes great care not to lose the quiet, even, forward impetus. When the horse maintains this, one can begin to ask rather more of it: but if it loses its impulsion, too much has been asked of it.

In this way, progress is made in small stages, each stage resulting from the previous one. In quite a short space of time, the horse will be totally obedient to the urging of the legs, and, resulting from the increased impetus from its hindquarters – a direct effect of this urging – it will accept a rein contact and begin to mouth the bit. The horse is induced to accept the rein contact by the rider's passive hands: it is necessary that the horse looks for the contact itself. This should not be accomplished by the rider's drawing back his hands, which could well make the horse draw its head back behind the vertical line, hunch itself and start playing with the bit. It must *never* be behind the bit or try to spit it out: this is to be avoided by driving it more positively forward and at a slightly brisker pace. If this is not successful, a tap with the whip is called for. If the rider hears the horse pushing the bit forward and playing with it, that, too, calls for a tap with the whip, accompanied by stronger forward-driving.

The quiet, regular pace must become more and more established. Such consolidation is the yardstick by which the rider judges whether his work is proceeding on the right lines. If, additionally, he seeks to influence increasingly with his back in the halts – and a calm, supple seat is an indispensable quality in this – and in the turns with appropriate shifting of his weight, the young horse will, after some time, be wholly obedient to the aids. When now the rider sits deeply and securely in the saddle and increases imperceptibly the influences of his back and legs, the horse will, of its own accord, come up to the passive hands. But any artificial or forced positioning of head or neck by pulling on the reins will be quite counter-productive. Arguably, this is a quicker way to make the horse *seem* to have that rounded neck that a schooled horse has, but in fact the horse has not learned obedience but has rather learned to evade the rider's influence by drawing in its neck and getting behind the bit.

Teaching a badly schooled horse to obey the aids
Correcting the faults of such horses is one of the most vital areas in riding. It teaches riders to work their horses actively and energetically, with feeling and patience. Riding such horses also teaches them to evaluate whether their attempts to influence are well or badly delivered.

It is the easiest thing in the world to spoil a well-schooled, sensitive horse by bad influences. If a rider has never or seldom had the opportunity of reschooling, let us say, a horse that goes behind the bit, he will not be in the best position

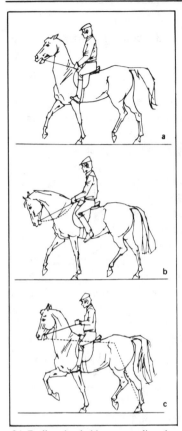

34 Badly schooled horses evading the aids:

a: Above or over the bit (stiff at the poll). The rider's hands are too low, his legs too far forward, and there is no co-ordination of his influences.

b: The sketch shows only that the horse is moving without pace or rhythm; close observation would be necessary to show if the rider is putting too much into his weight of rein (which would make his horse lean on the bit) or has no contact with the rein (when the horse would go behind the bit).

c: Ewe-necked, with a hollowed back; staccato steps that are too high; the horse raising itself without any accompanying collection or lowering of the hindquarters; in short, errors induced by the hands alone without the support of correct forward-driving influences.

to keep his horse constantly listening to the aids. His perception of when the horse is about to get behind the bit will not be sufficiently developed, nor will it tell him what measures to adopt. With a rider of this limited calibre, all horses will tend to present problems in the long term.

One talks of 'disobedience', but that term is totally inaccurate in this case. For the horse, while it does not respond to the influences attempted by its rider, does not do so out of stupidity or waywardness, but because it is experiencing fear or pain and its rider is not succeeding in making it understand what is required of it.

A horse has many ways of evading a rider's influences and there are many degrees of evasion. Almost inevitably it is the rider who is at fault, not the horse. This is certainly the case when a horse leans annoyingly on the bit, which is in most cases the result of heavy-handedness. One should try to rectify this by back-bracing and by driving the horse more positively forward and, if needs be, applying the spurs. But if the horse has accustomed itself to lean on the bit to the extent that it is using the hand as a prop, then the only remedy is a series of quick taps with the whip just behind the girth – and these will often need to be repeated if the horse shows signs of resting on the bit. It is also beneficial, immediately this happens, if the rider gives a single stroke of the whip as a punishment, but there must be no delay in this. The horse will then be startled into taking several steps forward at a quicker pace but will then resume its leaning. The punishment should then be repeated until the horse ceases this practice. However, the most effective remedy is not whip or spurs but the positive influence forward by back and legs.

A rider often complains that his horse:

has a hard, dead mouth

is stiff at the poll (in the case of highly strung horses)

gets above the bit

leans on the bit

jogs

has a wrong bend in the neck (behind the

third vertebra)

throws its head about (see martingale, p. 185)

is ewe-necked

gets behind the bit

draws itself in at the poll

hollows its back (in the case of highly strung horses with weak backs)

makes one or both hind legs stiff

takes short, over-hasty steps (in the case of highly strung horses)

goes crookedly

lets its tongue hang out

throws itself against the leg

loses its pace and impulsion

All these bad habits disappear immediately the horse is obedient to the aids. After all, they are symptoms of a basic defect – that of evading the aids – to which a horse has recourse in various ways.

No rider should think, then, that his horse has an innate, incurable defect, but do his very best to make his horse listen to the aids, otherwise a pattern of increasing problems is readily established.

Disobedience

SHYING

35 Shying and how to counteract it.

When a horse shies at a visible object, it turns its head towards that object, staring at it in fright. One should therefore turn the horse's head away from what is causing the shying, using leg pressure to push the quarters towards the object (see illustration 35). It is essential to act decisively to change the horse's position so that it cannot get itself into a state of rigid resistance. If the rider cannot succeed in urging the horse forward and changing its position, he is advised to dismount and lead his horse. A horse will be more likely to go past something frightening in the company of other riders and horses: in this case it is as well to turn the horse's head away before reaching the problem. Alternatively, it is often recommended that a rider, if he thinks fit, should let his horse have a good look at the fear-inspiring sight. He meanwhile speaks patiently and soothingly to the horse and tries to give it confidence and the horse may well come almost to 'interest' itself in what frightened it.

BUCKING

There are different kinds of bucking: the horse may simply buck in a forward direction, buck on the spot or buck with a twisting motion. Whichever it does, it will get its head down, from which position it can easily unseat its rider. The rider must counteract this by jerking movements with the reins to raise the horse's neck and head, at the same time pushing the horse forward in a positive manner. Unless he does this, the rider will almost certainly end up on the ground unless the horse chooses to stop bucking. Horses with tender backs are prone to buck just after they have been mounted, particularly if the saddle has been put on in a clumsy fashion. It will be evident that there is tension in its back when the horse is being led out to be mounted, for its back will look rigid and it will take nervous steps. It is best if such horses are lunged initially and walked around for some time until the stiffness has eased. It is most important that horses like this be very carefully saddled and the girth tightened gradually. Then, just a few seconds before mounting, one can loosen the girth by one or two holes. It is absolutely necessary to exercise the greatest care with these horses: it is all too easy for them to buck more and more if this is not done.

REARING

The remedy against rearing is the same as that for bucking – riding the horse forward – for it can only rear at a standstill. If the horse has surprised its rider by rearing, his best course is to hold on to the mane or, better still, hold on round the neck to avoid coming out of the saddle or overturning the horse completely by using the reins to stay on. It is also as well to take one's feet out of the stirrup-irons. Immediately the horse is level again, it should be ridden forward firmly with the rider releasing his grip on neck or mane. All too often, riders hang on to these far too long, so losing their seat and any chance of influencing the horse. When the horse is horizontal again, its neck and head should be raised, as a horse cannot rear if its neck is in the air. A rider should take this action if he feels that his horse is about to rear, but this is seldom something one can anticipate. One cannot prevent rearing by lowering the hands and exerting downward pressure.

The most serious consequence of rearing is the horse falling over backwards, which can happen if it loses its footing with both legs, or sideways if one leg gives way. The sole recourse is then to jump clear, but there is a danger – if this is done too soon – that one will not have got far enough away from the horse and will end up under it.

BOLTING

A horse is said to bolt if it rushes forward so strongly that its rider cannot bring it to a halt. This is usually caused by the rider pulling senselessly at the reins – and a horse will always win a tug-of-war. A horse can bolt quite efficiently with its head up and neck curved round. If a rider thinks he has lost control, there is no point in trying to apply the normal procedure for a halt or pulling on the reins. All he can do is look straight ahead and find enough open space for him gradually to turn the horse in a large circle, and slowly bring it to a halt by ever smaller circles. The inside rein is used almost exclusively, and riders are invariably surprised that a bolting horse can be turned so easily. It is most infrequent for a horse to bolt, with bloodshot eyes, totally out of all control.

PRESSING AGAINST THE WALL

When a horse presses itself against a wall or a tree, it curves its body around with its head away from the object and uses its inside legs to lean against it. The rider must act just as he does with

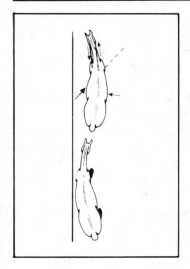

36 Pressing against the wall and how to counteract it.

a shying horse: he must effect a bend in the opposite direction. In this case, of course, the horse must be made to bend with its head towards the object it wants to lean against. This prevents the horse using its inside legs to keep itself there and the rider can use his inside leg to urge his horse forward and away from the object. The most important feature is that the horse is made to bend the other way (see illustration 36).

NAPPINESS

Nappiness is the term applied when a horse shows a disinclination to move from one spot, to leave other horses, to leave its stall or to move away from the door of the school. When asked to move on, it will rear or buck or try to press its rider against a wall. The method of correction is the same as that applied to bucking, rearing and pressing against a wall. It is most important in this case, however, to drive the horse forward.

Should the desire to stay with other horses or make its way back to its stall only manifest itself some time after a ride has been in progress, this is a definite indication that the horse is not listening to the aids. When a horse resists in this way, it is a warning for the rider to look carefully at this aspect of the horse's schooling.

HOW DOES ONE CORRECT BAD HABITS?

Riders often seek advice on the correction of these bad habits, and they hear much counsel concerning running-reins, lungeing-reins, cavaletti and suchlike. Most such advice is merely a palliative, something that may help without getting to the root of the problem: for example, one may be told to get the horse to mouth the bit or lower its neck. But this will not in any way help to achieve what is important, namely getting the horse so relaxed that it will do what its rider wants, will understand his influences and carry them out. It is not possible to find a remedy that works like the right kind of medicine – infallibly. Therefore a young rider who wants to reschool a badly schooled horse should not be in too much of a hurry. He should first get to know his horse and be able to accommodate himself to its movements: in other words, be able to sit deeply and securely in the saddle.

The procedure for correcting bad habits does not vary, for the objective is a fixed one: making the horse obey the rider, which is another way of saying listen to the aids. Certainly, a whole host of problems will be encountered: the horse may go behind the bit, may be above the bit, may make itself stiff in the poll, in the back or in its hind legs. But all correction must be applied to the whole horse, never just to certain parts of it. The steps always to be followed, then, are these:

1　The horse must first learn to go forward in response to the driving influences.
2　When it succeeds in this, it should be taught to bend towards the inside.
3　When that has been learned, it should be taught to stretch its head downwards.
4　From this position, it must be encouraged to accept the bit.
5　When it has freely accepted the bit, it is given collection by half-halts.

One should always use a snaffle in teaching a horse to accept the bit. It is gentler in action and the horse will accept it more readily.

How a badly made horse is taught to obey the driving influences
This problem is most severe with horses who bolt because they are running away from leg pressure. This leads many riders to believe that there is just no way to drive such horses forward. In these cases it is essential to calm the horse. It is advisable to trot in circles and, if that does not succeed, in small circles. The rider must not make the mistake of pulling on the reins to achieve a halt. At this stage they are used only to indicate direction. The circles or small circles must be persevered with until the horse will accept being driven forward without responding by bolting. The more successful one is at sitting deeply and quietly in the saddle, at bracing the back and using the legs sensitively against the

horse's sides, the more quickly this will be accomplished. But any kind of noisy leg movement will frighten the horse and send it rushing off once again. All horses gradually let themselves be lulled by continuous tight circling and there is simply no other means that may be employed. The rider will be surprised how quickly he can start to use driving influences but he will find this possible only if his seat is really deep and quiet.

This last point is of paramount importance in the case of horses who suffer from back pains: there must be no stiffness, no unfeelingness and the rider must sit deeply and with suppleness and with back braced. Nothing will be achieved if the rider adopts a position of leaning forward. The inside rein is used to keep the horse circling and the outside rein has no part to play at this stage; nor does one need to be concerned with the horse's general carriage. It is, though, important for the rider to dictate the pace, not let the horse decide. More thorough work begins only when the foregoing has been achieved. Dressage proper begins when the horse accepts the discipline, becomes lazy, as it were, and listens to the driving influences: that is the time for the rider to begin to use back and leg influence.

One adopts the reverse procedure with horses who are bored and will not listen to the leg. In these cases it is an error to attempt to drive solely with the legs. Spurs hurt such horses without achieving anything and increase their apathy. The remedy is the use of the whip (see p. 181) and this is equally applicable in the case of an unschooled horse. When reinforced with the whip, leg and back influences are obeyed by th horse and it will go forward. But it is essential that a rider knows how to use his whip before he attempts to use it to help make his horse obedient to the aids.

Once the horse has learned to go forward in response to back and leg pressure, the rider will soon find he can determine the working pace – one that is calm and regular but always just a little faster than the pace the horse would choose if left to its own devices. This last point is the one that is most frequently overlooked in the teaching of the aids.

Why and how a spoilt horse is worked in a flexed position

Once one has taught the spoilt horse to go forward in response to back and leg pressure, it must learn how to flex. Before a horse can be taught to obey the aids, it must be brought to a state of complete relaxation, and when this is accomplished, life will be that much easier for the horse.

All horses, particularly those with bad backs or with tensions in various parts of their anatomy, loosen up more readily when they are worked in flexion, that is to say with bending, than if they are worked in a straight line. As mentioned previously, a horse is born with some bias to left or right and is never completely straight. A rider should make his horse bend towards the inside by judicious pressure with the inside rein and giving with the other one. Most horses will quickly accept this and bend towards the inside. If they will not do this so readily on one side, they will on the other. It is up to the rider to find out on which rein his horse goes best, and this is done by changes of direction while carrying out circles or small circles. This is not difficult to assess and does not call for any great degree of riding skill. Work is commenced on the side on which the horse bends most readily. It is of no consequence whether the horse bends first at the neck and then behind, or the other way round, or simultaneously, as long as it is borne in mind that impelling the horse forward is the prime goal and that any neglect of a correct seat or any odd way of sitting may lead to failure to achieve this or to an apparent success that is a success only in superficial ways.

Should the horse refuse to bend to the inside on both reins, despite its rider's urging – and most horses will usually do this on one rein if the rider is sitting well into the saddle and is working carefully with the inside rein – the use of running-reins is the remedy (see illustration 37 and p. 185).

Using running-reins does complicate matters somewhat, but is sometimes unavoidable. It is essential, though, for the rider to understand the use of running-reins before using them. When they have served their purpose, they should immediately be discarded, as they might then do more harm than good. The quickest way to get the horse bending towards the inside is to use the inside rein very gently while allowing with the outside rein and riding the horse very definitely forward. But if the rider is too rough with the inside rein, he should not be surprised when his horse, who is much stronger than he, refuses to be pulled round and will not bend docilely. To be successful, it is most important to be very considerate of the horse's mouth, to move one's weight to the inside and to be sure to push the horse positively forward. If success is not forthcoming on one rein, the same procedure should be tried on the other, and if the bend does not come on the circle, then small circles should be tried. Changing the rein repeatedly is a useful process, but, when one does this, it is essential that, when one of the rider's hands becomes the outside one, he gives with it and does not hang on.

When the horse is bending correctly, the inside rein is used solely to maintain the bend and not to lose it. It is important to bear in mind that the more sensitive the inside rein, the more readily the horse obeys it.

Why and how a spoilt horse is taught to stretch its neck forward and downward
Many riders are puzzled by the necessity of obtaining a low head and neck carriage when the aim of the horse's schooling is to make it higher in front and lower behind. Raising the forehand is of value only when it is the result of achieving a lowering of the hindquarters (relative head-raising). The horse's quarters have to curve under it more and become lower to give it more propelling power (see p. 107). The quarters, then, to fit them for this work, need to be developed and strengthened. However, when a horse propels with its quarters, it naturally lowers its

head. But it must not just lower it: it must be made to stretch it, and the stretching is arguably more important than the lowering. If one does not cultivate the ability to make the horse stretch its neck, one will not be able to prevent it from lurching about without a rein contact, which means it will get behind the bit and evade the influence of the reins. The horse would then never be properly obedient to the aids.

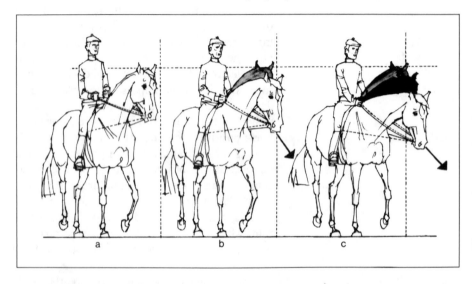

a   b   c

37 Teaching a horse how to stretch its head and neck forward and downward; this is being done while circling with running-reins.

b and c: Lowering and stretching the neck.

Teaching the horse to lower and stretch its neck is essential in encouraging it to loosen up in the back, in giving it collection and making it bring its hind legs further forward. The horse is now in a state of equilibrium. To achieve this, it is best to start on a circle or a small circle at a working trot. Initially the rider exerts a very slight pressure on the outer jaw and gives immediately with the same hand or forearm. The point of this momentary pressure is to draw the horse's attention to the outside rein. The giving that follows is the important factor, for it encourages the horse to relax and stretch its neck. Legs and braced back should ensure that the horse goes forward and always at a slightly faster pace than it would choose. If the rider neglects his prompting or the horse decides its own pace, it no longer feels any compulsion to take up the bit and the exercise is unsuccessful. Success is achieved when forward-driving is accompanied by a sensitive bringing forward of the outside hand and the horse is virtually enticed to stretch forward on a longer rein. The inside hand keeps the horse's bend and must not be used as a reinforcement for the outside hand. This is an important point, for riders must not get into the habit of using hands alternately to influence: they then tend to act in a to-and-fro motion with the hands, in other words, to saw. This would also mean that a horse would never be ready to listen to the aids: it would be behind the bit or leaning on it. If the rider succeeds in continuous giving with the outside hand and encouraging the horse to stretch its neck and take the bit, the horse will gradually perform as the rider would wish. It will come to regard the procedure as boring and pointless but in no sense painful or unpleasant. It will therefore not object and, as circling continues, will feel more comfortable and relaxed. If the rider maintains his patience, the horse will gradually reach forward towards the bit. Should the rider wish to speed things up, he can try the effect of giving the horse a little more bend and urging a little more strongly, raising the hands momentarily to increase the horse's contact with the strengthened outside rein. The more the horse, with its neck raised, feels the pressure in its stiff lower jaws, the sooner and more willingly it will look for the bit in a downward direction, simply because that feels more pleasant. The rider is well advised to experiment on the other rein as the horse might find that easier. But he should not try to do any more than this. He can only indicate the way a horse should stretch forward and downward: the horse must then work it out itself.

It should take most horses only a few minutes to get the idea. Some may take half an hour but, ultimately, all will react favourably to this yielding hand. And once the horse has, of its own volition, made a cautious attempt to stretch its neck, its rider should simply continue to keep it flexed to the inside and drive it forward with legs and back up to the outside rein. This should be carried out on both reins alternately, but initially, more attention should be given to the side on which the horse bends more readily, so that some progress is apparent and also because the horse will understand more readily what is required of it. Attention is then given to the other rein. The rider then changes the rein direction repeatedly until the horse goes absolutely evenly on both reins with neck stretched forwards and downwards. The basis is now established for the horse to obey the aids. Running-reins can be used profitably here but only in the hands of a skilled teacher, for their wrong use can cause untold harm (a false bend, dead mouth, tongue drawn aside).

How a spoilt horse stretches downwards and accepts the bit

As soon as a horse is happy to stretch its neck forward and downward on both reins, the rider has only to use the reins passively. The horse then takes up the bit and begins to mouth it. If it is being asked for nothing more than going forward briskly, it will not show any sign of stiffness, tension or fear. The neck-stretching is, then, to be regarded as an absolute prerequisite for the horse to find and accept the bit. However, stretching the neck must not be called accepting the bit, just as succeeding in obtaining flexion of the horse was not synonymous with the horse's extending its neck. But all these three requirements:

obtaining flexion

the neck extension

and achieving a contact with the bit

are very closely bound up with each other, far more than might appear on first reflection. It is, however, necessary to examine them separately to arrive at full understanding.

At all times it is important to bear in mind that the horse must be driven up to the bit and the outside hand must assure the rider that contact between the horse's mouth and the hands is really brought about by this driving and is not, perhaps, the result of pulling on the reins.

Stiffness and rigidity that may have been present in jaws, lower jaws, neck, back and legs

38 Lengthening the stride (a and b). Contrast this with false flexion (c).

should vanish when one adopts an even working trot that may be monotonous but is energetic. The horse shows an increasing degree of relaxation and finally listens to the rider's legs, back and reins. It is then in equilibrium.

How, when the horse accepts the bit, it will shorten its profile

If the foregoing work has been carried out successfully, the horse will be obedient to the aids. But it is necessary to consolidate the achievement. The horse must repeatedly be made to extend its neck so that this extension, which it can only find comfortable, becomes confirmed. The strides will now become even more regular and steady, and, as a consequence of positive forward-driving, will become longer. The back becomes supple, arching itself and flattening with each step, all muscles come into play and there is no hint of stiffness.

If the reins are drawn back slightly, the horse, although driven forward into a greater contact with the bit, will not just mouth the bit but will yield to the increased rein pressure, shorten itself without resisting – in other words, take more weight on its hindquarters – and come to a halt. Such action is a preliminary to work on collection (see p. 104).

What we have described will not bring about results with all horses in half an hour, but it will soon be apparent that it is the right way to success. It may take from eight to fourteen days for the rider to evaluate and master these lessons and he should then be able to train his horse to listen to the aids like a well-schooled horse in just a few days. But if the horse does not succeed in this in a short period of time, in all probability it will not succeed at all, and it will then be up to the rider to ask himself frankly if the fault is not, perhaps, his own. Inevitably, the root cause of failure is that the rider has never mastered the ability to accommodate himself to his horse's movements.

QUESTIONS, DOUBTS AND MISTAKES IN SUCH
CORRECTION

The prescribed method of teaching a spoilt horse
the aids appears simple in theory. And it is, in
practice, much simpler than people generally
think. The method ought to be known to every
rider, as it is necessary in developing feel. Anyone who has undertaken to teach a spoilt horse
to obey the aids should keep totally clear in his
mind that success is to be achieved only if he can
harmonise his own movements with those of the
horse and sit deeply and securely in the saddle. It
can be stated categorically that unless this is
mastered there is no possibility of making one's
horse listen to the aids, as correct influencing
cannot be applied.

People often ask if one should rectify bad
habits in a head-on manner or avoid a confron-
tation. The very form in which this question is
phrased is a wrong one. 'Head-on' suggests a
conflict involving brute force and strength,
whereas the correction of any fault demands
extreme concentration, intuition, understanding
and patience, with the rider hoping that, by
employing these, he will make his horse understand what is required and submit to his intentions.

Many riders believe that many a fault in their
horses, such as jogging and hollowing the back,
results from defects of character or conformation and is simply impossible to correct. But the
point must be made that human beings, if they
are handled incorrectly, can become contrary
and irritable.

Another common misapprehension is that the
hardest task one can undertake is to correct a
horse who goes behind the bit. Again, the fact of
the matter is that, if a rider has that deep, secure
seat and an instinct and experience in the
correcting of faults, there is no 'hardest task':
tasks differ only in the extent that the fault is
more or less deep-rooted.

One often hears the recommendation that the
horse should be made to obey the aids initially at

halt or in the walk, rather than at a trot, and that when this has been mastered, it can obey the aids at a trot. This is unsound advice, for this is a much more difficult way to set about things and invariably leads to the horse getting behind the bit. It is the pronounced forward motion in the trot that is so helpful to the rider in making plain to him that he is not just working on the horse's neck or head but on the horse as a whole. And it is far easier at a trot than at walk or halt to know whether the horse is reacting sufficiently to one's attempts to drive it forward and therefore whether it is going on properly or drawing back.

Another frequently heard piece of advice that is much misunderstood and is the cause of a very large number of faults is, 'The rider should give with his hands as soon as the horse gives.' What is really meant is that a rider should never remain fixed in a particular position, so shortening the reins should not last beyond the point at which a horse yields. If the rider continues his rein pressure after he has achieved what he set out to do, the horse, quite understandably, does not know what is wanted. The truly sensitive rider anticipates the horse's yielding and effectively yields his own pressure simultaneously.

The advice is often turned the other way round and equally wrongly comprehended: 'The rider should only yield after his horse has given.' In other words, he should pull on the reins until the horse has been made to give. Advice like this is a short-cut to mistakes. If the horse does not give the moment he feels rein pressure, the fault is invariably that the rider has not at the same time used sufficient back and leg influence, such as he would have to do in asking for a halt. It will often suffice to repeat the exercise or perhaps use stronger influences to achieve obedience from the horse. But if the procedure for halting, when carried out in a definite manner, does not have the intended effect, and the horse continues to lean or even leans more strongly, then the only recourse for the rider to bring about compliance in his horse is to get it to stretch its neck forward and downward. If he does not do this, but continues his rein pressure, the horse may stretch its neck forward and downward of its own accord, but any yielding that it does make will be a matter of luck and nothing to do with the rider's skill. The rider would have done nothing positive: he would merely have waited until the horse happened to yield. But usually it does not happen like this, and invariably a tugging match begins. If the horse should then momentarily cease pulling – and it is ten times as strong as a rider – the odds are 100 to 1 that the rider will miss the long-awaited moment and yield with his hands far too late. And, even then, if he should manage to take advantage at just the right moment, it is almost certain, as we have described earlier, that the horse will end up behind the bit.

Many riders are ignorant of back-bracing: they speak of 'back' but do not know how to make use of it. Others cannot see that it can have any influence. Others are not convinced of its effectiveness because they have never realised that one can push the horse's head forward as if it were at the end of two shafts so that the neck is lengthened; or it may be that they think that this exercise is so difficult that only the most highly accomplished equestrians can manage it. Many such riders do not trust themselves to give with the reins, not believing that they will manage to get the horse to round its neck once more, with the result that it will be out of control.

This attitude leads riders to try to keep their horses in check by pulling on the reins. They feel they will, by so doing, attain the flexed position in which the horse's head is almost vertical (see p. 107). Horses with any sense, however, resent this and the riders will therefore pull more strongly or saw with their hands. If the horses' reaction is then to give way and draw their heads back, their riders think they have achieved obedience and, as there is now no resistance in their hands, reward their horses with a pat, stop pushing them forward and, at a stroke, the horses are encouraged to get behind the bit. In no time they learn to bring their heads back and curve their necks in order to evade true rein contact. This happens countless times and is far more common than one thinks. The end result is that the horse both gets behind the bit and has a false bend; in other words, the horse bends at the neck instead of at the poll. This incorrect bend is easily recognised and is most ugly.

WHAT DO WE UNDERSTAND BY RIDING WITH COLLECTION?

People speak frequently of riding 'with collection', but we have deliberately avoided using the term, for its use can induce one to think that there is a particular outline that the horse can adopt which gives it the best possible carriage, and that one should strive to attain this. This notion is reinforced by the idea of achieving a flexed head carriage, the underlying thought being that collection depends principally on the way the neck and head are carried (see p. 107).

It has been pointed out several times previously that, whenever we have spoken of the real aim of the art of riding – harmonious rapport with the horse, with the least expenditure of effort on the part of the rider and the greatest care for the horse – we have emphasised that one gives aids to the *whole* horse. People pay lip service to this idea but far too often ignore it. They think they will find short-cuts to riding mastery. They think they can concentrate on working on one part of a horse at a time to cure stiffness or tension. They will work on the mouth by getting the horse to mouth the bit, and on the poll and lower jaws by bending and straightening; and such riders think they can achieve things by working on any one of their horse's legs. With such notions, it is all to easy to lose a sense of proportion. How can one construct a building without an overall sense of the complete plan?

The ideas of riding a horse with a rounded carriage or with collection lead most frequently to wrong thinking. They are correct in principle but are inevitably corrupted in practice. The horse is taught to round its neck, which makes the highest point not in the poll but roughly three hands further back. Its forehead is brought back behind the vertical line and this gives the horse a pleasing appearance. It may not be correct but at least it looks better than if the horse waved its neck and head in the air. The horse will usually feel quite comfortable and will take calm strides even though they are shorter than one would wish: it will not, however, have impulsion.

Inexperienced riders find such horses quite reasonable to ride both in the school and hacking out in countryside with which the horse is familiar. The horses do not use themselves to any extent and their paces show little elevation. Their riders will therefore be thrown upwards relatively little and will find things quite comfortable. (This is a good reason why horses on which beginners are taught should have side-reins.) Moreover, as a result of their earlier experience, such horses will have hard mouths and will not react particularly if their riders have recourse to hanging on now and again. But these horses can in no sense be called obedient, and they do suffer from the fact that it is never possible to get them collected. The low carriage of neck and head does not allow a lowering of the quarters and, if such a lowering were achieved, it would result in a greatly rounded back with the rider perched on the top of it.

Essentially, such horses are simply never obedient to the aids and do not give the rider anything he asks for that is outside their experience. This can make things most difficult for him and is especially noticeable if, for instance, he tries to turn his horse from other horses with whom he has been riding. His horse may stop, rear, kick out, refuse to turn, get behind the bit or lean so heavily on it that the rider has no control. The horse is now the master and can follow the other horses: above all, it does not execute its rider's wishes. Now is the time for the rider to take stock of himself and to reflect that it is high time he made his horse obey the aids: more often than not he will blame an innocent animal and give undeserved punishment. But the horse will not know why it has been beaten and will not be able to understand its rider's actions in the slightest. It has never been taught to leave the company of other horses; it has always been praised when it troops along with them with an apparently nicely rounded neck. It makes complete nonsense at such times to punish a horse with spurs or – and one sees this frequently – by pulling it about in the mouth.

The assumption that a fixed correct outline is what one wants to achieve in the horse brings with it a whole host of problems: the shape of the horse becomes an obsession. But it is not always so easy to differentiate between correctly teaching a horse the aids and riding with collection. Each rider should think out in advance what he is trying to do and try to carry out his project. But if some aspect seems to him to be difficult and its realisation uncertain, he often drops it from his scheme of schooling without much thought and makes do with an inferior performance. If he were honest with himself and admitted this omission, the damage would not be so great: sadly, the omission is often a subconscious one.

It may therefore be helpful if we touch on aspects of wrong-thinking in obtaining a good carriage. The procedure will vary greatly, depending on the difference in inclination and temperament of rider, instructor and horse. Some start with the horse at a pillar and equipped with side-reins which encourage it to mouth the bit. The reins at first act lightly and then more strongly as a rounding of the neck becomes apparent. Some work the horse in hand or on the lunge with side-reins adjusted in varying degrees. Others have the idea that they can teach the aids from the saddle with the horse at halt and obtain a rounding of the neck without using much driving influence. Sometimes a second person on foot tries misguidedly to obtain a mouthing at the bit or a rounding of the outline without the rider doing any driving. Sometimes, side-reins or running-reins are used to try to achieve a rounding of the horse's neck at halt or walk with the rider then urging it into a cautious trot to try to maintain the rounding.

Being a creature of habit, the horse tends to maintain a position and may comply. Its nose will come down and its mouth become more insensitive. The horse is a good-natured animal who wants to please the ingenious rider, who ends up by being well pleased that he has brought his horse into such an attractive shape.

The fear of some riders of pulling their horses in too hard and achieving an exaggerated bend, leads them to fall into the trap of dispensing with a steady contact between the horse's mouth and their hands and hence any possibility of the horse obeying the aids. It has to be admitted that many horses will go well over territory with which they are familiar and respond with apparent readiness to their rider's directional promptings. They will, however, always be on their forehand, will tire more quickly and their front legs will suffer more in the long term. And the rider will be unable to impose his will on his horse when necessity demands that he ask it to do anything out of the ordinary (see illustration 39).

Stage three in training

COLLECTION AND RAISING THE FOREHAND

Dressage properly begins when the horse has been taught the aids and is ready to obey them. To go comprehensively into such training is outside the scope of this book but every rider should understand fully its methods and aims. If the ultimate goal is not firmly in his mind, wrong measures may well be adopted. Dressage seeks to educate towards obedience and to increase performance and flexibility. Lessons should lead to a complete harmony between rider and horse in Haute Ecole. In such lessons one looks for improvements in responsiveness and collection and these form the yardstick by which one can judge whether work is on the right lines.

The greater the obedience the rider demands from his horse and the more rapid and complex the various movements that he hopes will be executed smoothly, the more the emphasis must be on controlling the horse's hindquarters, which are effectively its powerhouse. Because of the

39 Working a horse from the ground. It is instructive to watch a led horse moving freely. The centre of gravity seems to be much nearer the forehand than the quarters. The hind legs step well forward but in a flat manner and do not supply the means for collection. When a rider achieves collection, he will make the quarters bear a greater load and the horse will use its hind legs differently, bending the joints more and taking steps that are both more elevated and shorter.

way a horse is made, its large head and neck are supported more by its front legs than by its hind legs and this makes its centre of gravity nearer the front legs than the hind. Thus the former have a carrying role and the latter a propelling role. Flat-racehorses and jumpers and steeplechasers impose more strain on their front legs, as do carriage and draught horses, especially when pulling a heavy load. This becomes very clear if one looks at a horse ploughing or drawing a well-loaded cart.

In contrast, a dressage horse, and most certainly one that is to do Haute Ecole work, has to do rather more carrying than propulsion with its hind legs and has to get them well forward and under the centre of gravity. This is called collection, or collection on the hindquarters. The principle of collection is explained in illustration 40 and one can observe how, with an increase in the demands made on them, the hind legs come more and more forward under the centre of gravity until, ultimately, in the levade, they bear the whole weight.

Collection is achieved partly by training, such as bending the haunches (see illustration 40c) and sideways movements, particularly shoulder-

40 Collection and raising of the forehand. The dotted lines behind the horses show the increased rounding and lowering of the quarters.

a: Obedience to the aids but without collection.

b: With collection.

c: Engaging the haunches.

d: Piaffe.

e: Levade.

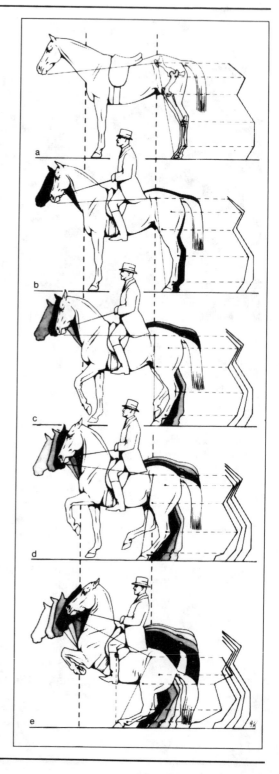

in, and partly, if more indirectly, by the overall training programme; and, of course, by every single half-halt that is asked for generally.

One finds that gradually, almost of its own accord, the horse shortens its profile from rear to front, with the hind legs working more actively under the centre of gravity and the quarters lowered. The horse is therefore not just more attentive and ready to put its whole effort into carrying out the slightest instruction from its rider, but it makes a better and prouder impression – it has more presence. This is why, at all times, artists have depicted horses in a state of collection when they wish to represent them in full majesty. Many examples come to mind, monuments such as the Parthenon frieze, the Pergamon altar of antiquity, the wonderful statue of Prince Eugene in front of the Imperial Palace in Vienna. In the field of painting, Velazquez and David tended to depict horses in the levade.

A natural corollary to the lowering of the quarters is that the forehand, bearing less weight, is raised. The hind legs show a more elevated action which makes the paces shorter (relative raising). One can contribute to this process by using the hands (absolute raising) and, simultaneously, the back and legs energetically to bring about further raising of neck and head, which has the effect of displacing the centre of gravity a little backwards towards the hind legs. It is, however, important that the driving influence be definite and effective, otherwise an unwanted hollowing of the back will result (see illustration 48).

When collected, the horse shows an increased bend in its poll and neck, and this should develop naturally when the horse who is obeying the aids is taken up or collected by a series of half-halts. It should not be regarded therefore as a lesson in its own right. If done too energetically by the rider, it can result in the horse being above or behind the bit (see illustration 34) or bent wrongly behind the third neck vertebra.

Care must also be taken in collection and raising not to try to achieve the idealised outline of a perfect shape — something that we warned against in the advice on making a horse obey the aids. It is all too easy to fall into this trap, especially if one pays too much attention to individual details. It takes a long time to achieve collection and the raising of the forehand in a horse, as it is strenuous for it and could impair its soundness. It may certainly require a year or two's work and possibly even longer, depending on the degree of dressage to which one aspires.

First of all one must prepare the hindquarters to bear the increased load by training and strengthening them. If this work is hurried, the horse may suffer pains leading to stiffness, over-exertion, pulled muscles, inflamed tendons and windgalls, and, in extreme cases, lameness which could be so severe as to make the horse unfit for such work.

The remarks we have made on making a horse obedient to the aids apply even more in the case of teaching it collection. It should also be pointed out that the collected horse makes an impression at once more energetic, cooperative and obedient. It carries out the most difficult commands in the most lively manner, with impulsion but as one with its rider and with the onlooker being unable to notice any apparent aid being given.

41 Extended trot. Eva Maria Pracht on Gemma.

42 Medium trot. Dr Reiner Klimke riding Mehmed.

43 Passage. Dr Josef Neckermann riding Venetia.

It will never be possible to judge the degree of collection of a horse by looking only at the carriage of neck and head or by the fact that a lowering of the quarters has been achieved. Judgement can only be made by watching closely the performance of a horse while it is being ridden. The illustrations show clearly that the

amount the quarters are lowered is minimal at halt (see illustration 40) and, in motion, even at passage, so infinitesimal that one is almost unaware of it (see illustration 47).

A horse with good conformation, when walking out, should place its hind hooves some twenty centimetres in front of where its front hooves were placed. This can easily be observed when the horse is being led or is walking in the paddock, for it is the normal action of an un-collected horse (cf. illustration 39). With increased collection, when, due to the decreased weight on the forehand, the steps become more elevated and shorter, the hind legs cease coming further forward than the forelegs. (This is shown clearly in illustration 47.) But it must not be assumed that the fact that the hind legs are making shorter steps is a proof that good collec-tion has been attained. Horses going without impulsion, badly schooled horses and those with hollow backs move like this. It is never wise to make rash decisions on the basis of a single detail or an incomplete view.

At faster paces, certainly at a strong trot, one often notices a horse striking its foreleg shoes with its hind ones. This, and a horse putting its hind legs down too far to the sides, is an indica-tion either that it is being allowed to go on too fast for its degree of training or that it is getting tired.

Ordinary collection

By this term we understand a degree of collec-tion suitable for hacking out. A horse can use a greater or lesser degree of collection at any pace. The greater the degree, the more elevated will be its steps. This makes more demands on it and, of course, the length of the steps is less. Clearly, it is wise to conserve the horse's energies on longer rides and ask it for longer, flatter strides. And one can, at any time when necessary, ask the horse for more collection. Over difficult terrain – ground with many holes, hilly country or well-wooded country, one will ask the horse for a degree of collection similar to that which would be required in the school.

44 Working trot with the horse obeying the aids but without collection. Young horse being schooled. Note the still immature muscle-structure of this young horse as compared with that of the fully schooled dressage horse (illustration 46).

45 Collected trot. Experienced horse of the Spanish Riding School, Vienna.

46 Piaffe (High School). Extreme collection shown in this movement calling for trotting on the spot. Note how clearly the quarters are lowered so that they may come further forward and take more weight. Rosemarie Springer riding Lenard.

Dressage collection

By this term we understand, in contrast to an ordinary working collection, an increased degree of collection. Ordinary working collection and dressage collection are relative terms – relative in the sense that they will vary according to the differing conformations of different horses. As few riders can judge the degree of collection of their horse by its overall performance, by the lowering of its quarters and by changes in its steps, they have in mind a lesser or greater degree of flexion or bend of the neck. Some horses have such well-made necks and backs and are wonderfully suitable for dressage and school purposes that an ordinary collection in them would appear to be a dressage collection in a cobby horse with a short, thick neck.

The difference in elevated and flatter paces which one observes with increased collection is shown in illustration 40 on p. 106.

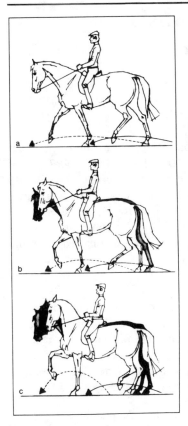

47 As increased collection is achieved in the trot, the steps become shorter and more elevated. Impulsion and cadence must remain unimpaired.

a: Working trot.
b: Collected trot.
c: Passage.

Self-collection

This term implies an apparent independent maintaining by the horse of a particular carriage or position that its rider has asked it for. It has nothing to do with a particular degree of collection or outward appearance. A horse that is obedient to the aids will soon achieve this self-collection as dressage training proceeds. And the more subtle the rider's aids and the more refined his rein influences, the sooner he will manage this.

The opposite side of the coin of self-collection is leaning on the bit. But self-collection is only an apparent quality: a horse who seems to have it still requires the driving seat of its rider and his passive hands. And self-collection is only truly present when rider and horse are completely in accord. However, horses who are behind the bit give the appearance of being in a state of self-collection. It is most difficult to distinguish right from wrong and very difficult to acquire a feeling for it. The moment a rider loses the ability to make his horse stretch its neck, it is behind the bit.

The only horses who can achieve self-collection are those who through correct and thorough training have built up their back and neck muscles to the extent that they carry themselves automatically under their rider. It follows then that self-collection is not to be expected of a young horse.

In the natural order of things there are horses who are clearly ideal for riding purposes and others who are hopeless. As a generalisation, the set of the neck and conformation of the neck musculature are the important criteria. The better the set of the neck and its muscle structure on the withers and shoulders, the better the riding horse. Horses with poorly made or badly set-on necks will seldom achieve self-collection.

CHAPTER THREE
The Lessons

The term 'lessons' is applied to all exercises that serve to increase the suppleness and obedience of the horse. At the same time, each lesson will help the rider to improve his sense of feel to a degree that will give him an ability to give aids so sensitively that they will not be apparent to an onlooker. We shall speak of 'suppling' exercises and 'collecting' exercises.

Exercises to improve suppleness

It is perfectly possible to lead a horse out of its stable and ride it immediately but one should not expect to get much concentration from the horse or any great degree of collection. After all, the horse, like any other animate being, needs a certain amount of limbering up. This is called suppling or relaxing.

The amount of time that will be necessary depends on the horse's temperament and conformation. Some horses need the briefest period of time; others may need two, five or ten minutes. For this loosening-up process, the brisker paces with the rider sitting lightly are recommended. In the rising trot, the rider should put his weight on his stirrup-irons and stand for the length of time it takes for the next pair of diagonals to make contact with the ground; he then returns to the saddle lightly but with his back braced and rises again immediately. In other words, he keeps coming back to the saddle every time on either the left or right diagonal. We say that the rider is trotting on the right or left hind leg. In the school, the rider always rises on the inside hind leg, and, when he changes the rein, he will, of course, rise on the other hind leg. A horse that finds it difficult to loosen up is best worked at a strong canter, over cavaletti or low jumps. Horses who would get excited by this should be given quiet, systematic bending work (see pp. 81, 121, 142). Once the horse shows, through well-executed half-halts, that it is listening to the aids, this exercise has served its purpose.

Collecting exercises to improve obedience

Collecting exercises, for example halts and shoulder-ins, are those lessons designed to stimulate the action of the hindquarters, and, by encouraging the horse to bring its hind legs further forward towards the centre of gravity, to make them bear more of the load. The key point to note is that all such exercises should be carried out with adequate back and leg influence.

It will take time for the novice to manage this but he should read the following lessons carefully, for they indicate the only correct method and they will tell him how his horse should react. They will also show him how the influences work in harmony and how they will bring the horse to a condition of collection.

The aids for walk, trot and halt

The aids for walk, trot and halt, which are intimately bound up with each other, should not be discussed separately. In all of them, one must:
brace the back
apply equal leg pressure with both legs
yield with the hands – keep them still – or take up the rein.
Clearly, the rein action is the decisive factor. The aid for walk bears roughly the same relationship to halt as it does to the aid for turning left. Walk, trot and halt should be carried out with the horse moving in a straight line. The rider must use both legs and both reins evenly. If one leg acts more strongly, or the weight in the reins varies, a one-sidedness will be caused which will make the horse deviate from the straight. On the other hand, if the horse has some element of one-sidedness, it may be necessary to use uneven pressure on one side or the other to keep it straight. It is absolutely essential to practise walk, trot and halt with the horse pointing completely straight ahead.

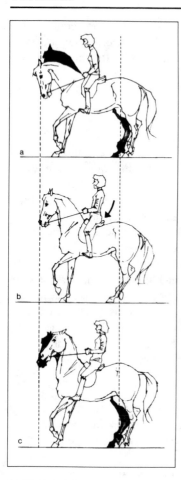

48 The halt (cf. illustrations 29 and 12).

a: Wrong: hands are too low and horse is on the forehand.

b: Correct: back and both legs are acting together.

c: Wrong: legs are not acting and the position is over the horse's back.

All riders learn to walk on and trot on in their very first lessons. They may well have had to add whip or voice to their efforts then to make the horse go forward, but they should now begin to feel that relatively little pressure is needed when they have acquired the skill to use back influence. Later still, practising trot on from halt will be an especially instructive experience for them, for here, a most basic fact becomes important: that an aid must never be something that takes a horse by surprise, but should be given with a gradually increasing pressure. If one acts with too much force, the horse will almost certainly canter on instead of trotting on. Halting is a more difficult art than walking on or trotting on. The horse, impelled forward by its rider's back and legs, comes up against the resistance of the passive reins even if there is no movement backward by the hands: this is logical, for the horse is being asked to go forward but the hands do not allow this. The horse shortens its profile towards the front, placing more weight on its hindquarters, and becomes lower behind and higher in front, the pace becomes slower and the strides more elevated.

Things are made more difficult for the novice rider in that, very likely, he was wrongly instructed initially to make his horse halt by pulling on the reins: at that time he would not have been familiar with back-influencing and if he had been told to execute a halt by using back and legs, he would simply not have known how to go about it. Stopping a horse by a pull on the reins is a habit that is very difficult, subsequently, to break. The rider does not see why he should now be asked to stop his horse in a different way.

It does, in fact, seem paradoxical to halt a forward movement by driving the horse forward. But if one does not do it this way, one is acting contrary to the most basic truism in riding, namely that one directs one's efforts to the whole of the horse and not to its mouth alone. In the case of well-behaved, older horses, success is possible with reins alone, but young or strong horses will not comply, being, quite simply, stronger than any human. Moreover, this method will not give perfect control over any horse. It will react by shaking its head and leaning on the bit and, when it does consent to halt, will do so on the forehand, lurching forward on to its front legs and doing its joints harm in the long term. It may, of course, not consent to halt but take it into its head to take off.

One cannot therefore over-emphasise how important it is for the young rider to learn very early on how to use his back and legs in asking for halt. And it is equally important that, when the horse has come to a halt, it is not allowed to step backwards. Horses like to do this, especially if they have halted in response to rein pressure only, but they will also do it if the rider, satisfied with his successful halt, takes his legs away from the horse's sides. Halts differ from half-halts. The former bring the horse to a standstill from any of the paces, while the latter serve to slow the tempo[1] at a particular pace or change the pace to walk. The term half-halt may also be applied to an influence that, without changing the pace, causes an increased degree of collection and a more elevated action in the horse. If a half-halt is not successful, that is, if the horse does not obey or does so incompletely, it must be repeated. Similarly, a halt is often executed inadequately and this should be repeated until success is achieved. The degree of emphasis that is made when asking for both halt and half-halt is determined by the sensitivity of the horse and there is no essential difference in the way the horse executes these.

Clearly, one has to ask more decisively – perhaps one should say, ask more often – for a halt from an extended trot, than one would in asking for a half-halt to bring the horse from a medium to a collected trot. On the other hand, the degree of emphasis is greater – or more frequent – in asking for a half-halt to go from medium trot to walk than it is in asking for halt from walk. It is therefore recommended that a

---

[1]By 'tempo' we mean covering a particular distance in a certain period of time (speed). It is essential that the cadence stays the same in the different tempi.

horse be asked for a half-halt as a preliminary to its being asked to carry out anything different, such as a change of direction or tempo. In effect, one is saying to the horse, 'Listen now!', and all these half-halts are asked for in the same manner, by driving the horse forward from behind up to the unyielding hands. The more often a horse is asked for this, the more attention it will give its rider and the more control the latter will have. And the rider will gradually find he can refine the action until, ultimately, he needs only to 'think' half-halt, and automatically brace his back, for his horse to listen attentively.

A novice rider should not get into his head that this sort of mastery over his body and that of the horse is to be achieved by just a few exercises. It is a matter of total patience that requires practice for days, weeks, months, even for years before success is necessarily achieved. The more neatly, subtly and sensitively a half-halt can be carried out, the more intimate is the relationship between rider and horse and the more perfect will the halts be. At the same time, the rider will find his seat improves, he will accommodate himself increasingly to his horse's movements, he will give aids more smoothly and they will not be perceptible to the onlooker.

The rein-back

The aid for rein-back is similar to those for walk on, trot on and halt. The back and legs impel the horse forward, but the reins oppose this, causing the horse to step backwards just at the moment when it is prepared to move forward. It is an error to pull at the reins without acting with the legs. There should not be a pull on the mouth, rather the whole of the horse should be brought to move backwards.

If the horse refuses to step back when this aid is given, it is not listening to the aids and must first be taught to respond to forward-going aids. Each rein-back must be preceded by a half-halt.

One should also keep very clear in one's mind just how many steps back the horse is to be asked to make, whether one, two, three or four. And one should then only carry out the number

49 The walk with a rein contact. In a properly carried-out walk, the sequence of steps is that they follow each other diagonally: right hind, right fore, left hind, left fore (four distinct paces).

50 The walk on a long rein is a way of judging the horse's relaxation and whether he is on the bit. It must not be confused with the walk in which the rein has been given away when there will be no contact with the horse's mouth at all.

planned. A rider who neglects this has invariably forgotten that the rein-back is controlled by his driving influences and is, most likely, pulling on the reins.

51 The rein-back. In this the horse steps backward on diagonal pairs of legs simultaneously. In this photograph the right diagonal is to the rear while the left diagonal prepares to leave the ground (two beats).

A horse who is correctly obeying the rein-back will show no resistance in the form of head-shaking, head-raising or lowering, pressure on the bit or moving its hindquarters to the side. If it should show any of these, the rider has proof that his influences have not been sensitive and clear, or that his horse was not obedient to the aids.

It is an especially useful exercise, immediately the last step back has been taken, to ask the horse to go forward without actually halting.

The rein-back is the most searching and also the most revealing test of the balance between driving and restraining influences. It should therefore only be attempted when one has satisfied oneself that the halt has properly been mastered.

Walk and trot

Much explanation is usually given as to the sequence of steps in the walk and trot. We shall restrict ourselves in this chapter but do emphasise that it is necessary for a rider not simply to walk or trot in any old manner but to retain an awareness at all times and to ride at a particular tempo and with a constant cadence.[1] There are differences in the walk: there is a free walk *on a loose rein* and there is a walk *on a rein* or with *a long rein*. We differentiate between ordinary walk, collected walk and extended walk.

In the trot we differentiate between working trot, collected trot, medium trot and extended trot.

The rider should take care to make frequent changes of tempo. All too often he has it in mind that he should continue to maintain a particular tempo in the trot and not fall into the error of letting his horse go at an undefined pace of its own choosing. If, at any time, the horse slows down, it is always the rider who is at fault in not paying attention.

Rather the rider should display industry and energy in riding his horse forward at a tempo that he chooses. The criticism can often be made of an otherwise adept rider that he lets his horse go forward 'any old how'. This means, in effect, that he is giving too much with his hands. But the criticism is only just if he has omitted to continue to drive forward. If he does continue to drive – and most riders do not – then he is not riding in a negligent manner.

Riding in a flexed position

A horse is said to be straight if its spinal column from poll to tail shows as a straight line. If there is a bend to one side or the other, this is called flexion. It is flexion to the left if the centre of gravity of the theoretical circle of which the bend forms part is to the left, and flexion to the right if the centre of gravity is to the right. The side on which the centre of gravity lies is called the inner side and this has nothing to do with whether this

[1]Each pace has a cadence: by this we mean the regular sequence of paces or jumps, tempo not being important. A collected tempo is often called a shortened tempo. This is incorrect, for a shortening would lead to dragging, tired steps. In a condition of collection, the steps should be lively and elevated (cadenced).

point is towards the centre of the school or not. Obviously then, if one is riding on the left rein, flexion may be to the left, but if one is riding on this rein with flexion to the right, the inner side is on the right.

The lateral curvature, which should affect evenly the whole of the horse's body, starts at the poll and continues through the neck and ridge of the back. This curvature reaches its maximum when the horse can accommodate itself in a circle with a diameter of six paces. A horse can, however, take up a crooked or irregular position and even an S shape so that the bend does not flow from poll round to tail. Regular lateral flexion can only be attained by a rider whose horse is listening to the aids.

There is much obsession with flexing and too much time is spent on it. The main point in riding is to make progress in a forward direction and it is therefore logical to devote most of one's efforts towards this. For this reason, young riders should be advised to practise riding straight forward and to try to develop their ability to tell when their horse is going perfectly straight.

Of course, when making turning movements and at the canter, the horse will have to deviate from the straight and, at some point, a rider will have to take into account the aspects of riding in a flexed position (see illustration 18, p. 44). The correct way to do this is fairly complicated because the rider must bring into play the influences of his back, weight, both legs and both reins all at the same time and yet be able to dictate a left or right bend to the horse. He has to know what he is doing with his seat-bones and hips, knees and heels; he must make correct displacement of his weight and must avoid collapsing his hips. It will take time for a rider to be able to manage all this. Only when he can correlate his influences in making turns on the spot (turning on the forehand and on the quarters) can he be said to have mastered the art of making his horse flex. Even though one may have a theoretical grasp of how the influences work, patience will be needed for one to acquire real feelings for them.

The rider's inside leg is the support or pivotal point. While it acts in a passive or supportive way, it must remain in contact with the horse: without it, it is not possible to achieve flexion. And all the other influences would then have the effect only of pushing the horse over to one side.

First phase: One asks for a half-halt.

Second phase: The horse starts to bend around the fixed point formed by the rider's inside leg. The centre of gravity begins to move to the inside. The inside hip and inside seatbone are pushed forward. The inside heel and inside knee are lowered. The outside leg pushes the hindquarters to the inside. The inside rein is shortened slightly. The outside rein gives slightly. If the horse has been listening to the aids it will now stretch the outside of its neck to maintain contact with the corresponding rein. This slight yielding by the rider of his outside rein is made solely by his turning his shoulders slightly to the inside without there being any bend at his hips. The outer rein can also be yielded slightly by a small turning of the wrist which brings the little finger slightly towards the horse's mouth.

Third phase: As soon as a little flexion has been achieved, the outside rein is taken up again. Now the horse has bent its neck, its action will be along the chord of the arc, in other words to increase the bend, and the outside rein will also press against the curve of the neck. It would be wrong to press the outside hand across the withers. Pressure is maintained with the rider's back, weight, both legs and inside rein.

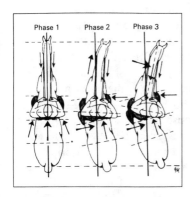

52 The aids for flexing to the right. The three stages should be carried out almost as one smooth movement.

The most significant influence is the displacement of the weight which acts in a similar way to what happens when a cyclist leans inwards, making a turn more by body displacement than by turning the handlebars. If one did not use this influence, the whole operation would not work so smoothly, for it is essential that the rider keep his centre of gravity over that of his horse. It is logical that if one makes a horse bend in a curve over its whole length, its centre of gravity moves inwards. When it bends around the rider's inside leg, the rider must sit so as to accommodate this, i.e. with seat-bone and hip pushed forward, inner leg just behind the girth and outer leg taken back about a hand's width behind the girth.

It is difficult to know, with the rein influences, which is more important in the second phase above – lengthening the outer or taking back the inner rein. Much depends on the degree of training of the horse and its sensitivity. It will not be possible for the rider to use only the inside rein to obtain good flexion. All horses will object in time to influencing in this way. With young and high-spirited horses, the giving with the outside rein is certainly more important than the shortening of the inside one.

In the third phase above, when a definite flexion to the inside has been achieved, both reins are taken up, the outer more so than the inner, for the latter now acts gently, simply maintaining contact, while the former instructs the horse as to position and reinforces and increases the flexion. Insensitive use of the inside rein is more likely to bring about resistance and bad habits such as head-shaking, than too strong a use of the outside one. If the horse does shake itself at the neck or poll, refuses to bend, rushes forward or backward, throws its head about or moves off the track, the rider must ride it forward and make it listen to the aids.

It is more difficult for the rider to know how he is doing in riding in a flexed position than in most other exercises. Even if mirrors are available in the school, the most common faults in riders are exaggerations in their seat and collapsing at the hip. Such riders will serve their cause best if they practise riding in a flexed position in circular movements, small circles, serpentines, in cantering and in turning on the spot, in particular the turn on the hinquarters. Practice of this sort will lead them to good flexion and how it should feel.

One is often wrongly advised to bring the outside shoulder back when riding in a flexed position. The thinking behind this is that most people are so stiff that, when they do this, they also bring the outside hip back. But this is wrong thinking, since what is wanted is that the inside hip should go forward and that is not at all the same thing as taking the opposite hip backward. That apart, everyone should be able to move hips and shoulders independently of each other and should have developed their relaxation to the extent of managing this. If a rider is too stiff, one will only make him more so by such outlandish advice. When riding in a flexed position, the outside shoulder must not be taken back; on the contrary, it must be pushed forward very slightly. This keeps the horse's head straight in front of the rider at a right-angle to the line made by his own shoulders (cf. illustration 56, p. 131).

Counter-flexion is the term used when flexion is the opposite of what it normally would be on a particular rein, i.e. a bend to the left on the right rein and vice versa. A counter lesson is an exercise in counter-flexion. Riding with counter-flexion and all lessons based on counter work are of great value because they oblige the horse to do things that are contrary to its natural way of going. The rider simply has to tell the horse what he wants with the utmost clarity and use his influences to exactly the right degree, for, in work of this kind, the horse will not help him by anticipating what is going to be asked of it as it tends to do in the more conventional exercises.

Turns on the spot

Turns on the spot are indispensable preparations for riding in a flexed position, turning, circling and cantering on. It is only with his horse at halt that a novice rider can learn how to influence, whether to left or to right: when his horse is in motion he has to concentrate too much on problems of balance and seat. But at halt, he can concentrate on how he gives influences and the degree of emphasis, and how the horse will react to them. In fact these exercises should commence in the very first riding lesson. Once the rider has acquired a feeling for these lateral influences, he will be able to apply it later on when asking his horse to flex.

It is, however, imperative that practising turns on the spot should be carried out in a step-by-step manner: after each step the rider should try to evaluate if the step just made was well or badly executed. This is the only way he will develop a feeling for it, and this is the only way in which he will be able to work out whether his influences led to success and whether or not they were imparted with the right degree of emphasis and coordination. If a rider should try to take several successive steps in this exercise, he will deprive himself of an ideal way of sharpening his sense of feel and will never achieve mastery of flexing his horse in motion.

One may divide turns on the spot into those made on the forehand and those on the hindquarters. It is generally considered that the latter are more difficult. Many people are therefore afraid of them and avoid practising them. And they are invariably started at too late a stage. The rider has to be able to execute perfect turns to both sides on the spot before he will be able to ride an accurate small circle in motion or get his horse to flex correctly for canter on.

TURNS ON THE FOREHAND

In turning on the forehand, the horse executes a turn around one of its forelegs: the right foreleg when turning to the right and the left foreleg when turning to the left. This movement demands that the horse be flexed or bent appropriately, i.e. to the right for right turns (see illustration 53). Turning on the forehand is considered only of marginal benefit in the schooling of a horse, for it shifts the weight from the quarters and puts the horse on its forehand. But it does serve a purpose in that it is a useful test of whether the horse is obedient to the leg. And it is of great benefit to a novice rider as a basic exercise in developing his sense of feel and as a good preparatory stage towards turns on the hindquarters. It is not at all necessary that the horse describes a complete circle every time and it is a

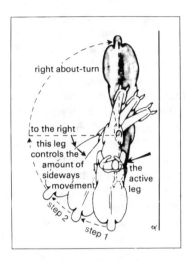

53 The turn on the forehand.

useful exercise if, from time to time, the horse is made to take two or three steps around and then to retrace them exactly. Turning on the fore-hand always starts by the rider asking his horse for half-halt to get its attention and also so that he himself can make sure his seat is correct. He then asks his horse to flex in the direction of the turn. This will certainly cause problems initially, for it is just these very turns that are best at showing a rider how to make his horse flex. The rider next applies pressure with his inside leg closely behind the girth, asking the horse's quar-ters to move sideways a step. The outside leg should be about a hand's width behind the girth and is used to control the sideways movement by limiting its extent. The horse should stand quite still between steps, enclosed, as it were, by the rider's two legs and the reins.

A rider should go no further than this until he is capable of analysing whether the step was made correctly and whether his influences were clear and given with the right amount of strength.

In turning on the forehand with opposite or counter-flexion, the horse is made to bend to-wards the side towards which the hindlegs will be made to turn. Now, it is the outside leg, in contact about a hand's width behind the girth, that brings about the turn. The inside leg con-trols the extent of the step. This particular exer-cise should not be attempted by a novice rider, being more appropriate for the rider who has progressed somewhat: its application is as an instructive aid for riding with counter-flexion, something that is required in Elementary dressage tests.

Many riders act with their hands subcon-sciously and this is made apparent by the horse's shuffling backward, shaking its head and dis-playing other kinds of resistance. The horse must not take any step forward or backward: if it wants to step forward, it must be prevented from doing so; if it wants to shuffle backwards, the rider must use the forward-driving pressure of back and legs to keep it quite still in one place.

It is very instructive for the rider not simply to

stimulate sideways movement with one leg when carrying out turns on the forehand, he should experiment using both legs unequally. He should try starting such a movement with one leg and curtailing it with the other. He can also ask for it with the one leg and prohibit it totally by counter-pressure with the other leg. Feeling will best be developed by learning from the inter-action of the bodily forces at one's disposal. At the same time, the opportunity can be taken of improving the leg position. In fact, turns on the forehand can only be executed if the legs are in contact with the horse. Unless a rider realises the effect that leg pressure makes, or if he neglects to test its effectiveness repeatedly, he will never develop a good leg position. On the other hand, a rider who develops his sensitivity to a degree that enables him not just to know when his horse has executed a step well but to know *in advance* that it is going to do so, will have adequate aware-ness of his leg position. He will be able to build on this awareness and will not need to be told by instructors whether his legs are properly positioned or not. This factor alone justifies the importance of forehand turns in the education of the rider.

TURNS ON THE HINDQUARTERS

In turning on the hindquarters, the horse executes a turn around one of its hind legs. It must flex appropriately, that is with a bend to the right for a right turn and a bend to the left for a left turn. Turning on the hindquarters is beneficial in the schooling of a horse as an intro-duction to turning corners, to sharp half-turns, to collection and to all lateral movements. For the rider, the benefits are that they develop his ability to feel the horse's movements and co-ordinate his lateral influences.

The first three steps of this turn are more easily executed than those that follow. This is because the horse is content to turn its body around its stationary inside hind leg for these initial steps, but then, when the turn is about one-third completed, this leg starts to feel un-

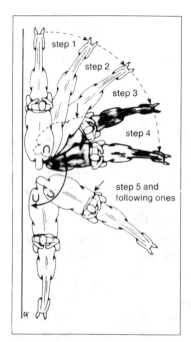

54 The turn on the hindquarters. The critical points are shaded.

comfortable and the horse tries to rectify this by stepping to one side or backwards. Clearly the rider will have fewer problems with these first three steps and it is as well, therefore, if initially he is allowed to practise just one, two or three steps. After every such move, the horse is brought back into the original position, step by step in the opposite direction and flexed correctly.

One starts off the turn with a half-halt with the horse perfectly straight; it is then flexed, and, to initiate the turn proper, the rider sits correctly for it with his weight towards the inside and the inside seat-bone pushed forward, his inside leg on the girth and his outside leg approximately a hand's breadth behind it. The outside rein and the outside leg cause the horse to turn around its hindquarters by increased pressure. The inside rein keeps a gentle contact and its task is to maintain the horse's flexion. The inside leg controls the extent of the steps and prevents the horse from taking more than one step at a time.

The horse is required to stand still between each step, imprisoned, as it were, between the rider's legs. A rider should assure himself after every step that the execution was correct, that his influences were delivered in accord with each other and with the right degree of firmness, and only then ask for the next step. If the horse steps forward or shuffles backwards – a worse fault – if it throws its head about or shows any other kind of objection, its rider has almost certainly disturbed it unwittingly when influencing. It is wrong thinking to believe that one will then be able to quieten the horse by taking one's legs away from its sides or giving away the reins. The correct procedure is to make the horse listen to the aids by using back and both legs and not to attempt the next step until it is standing calmly in a position from which it can respond to any aid.

Once the rider has achieved the ability to make his horse turn three steps around his quarters and back again, he can attempt the next steps. The outside leg has to work more actively than it did at the beginning of the movement, for the horse will try more strongly after the third or fourth step to move its quarters to the outside. The inside leg must allow the horse gradually to turn its quarters in the direction of the turn, as indicated by the long curved arrow in illustration 54.

The inside leg still has to ensure that each step is a separate one and to limit its extent and the horse must not be allowed to turn slowly and continuously around after the fourth step; each step should be a definite one with a brief interval intervening.

It is a total misconception that the horse can be pulled around by use of the inside rein.

When one has achieved a correct turn with correct use of both legs and reins, the horse should be standing in a straight line on its original hoof marks, and it should not be allowed to shuffle backwards.

Developing a turn on the hindquarters from walk is an instructive exercise. Although a rider may not have progressed to the stage at which his horse listens to the aids at halt, he can utilise the horse's forward impetus when asking for halt and making the first of the turning steps at the same time. He will still have to be able to apply influence on one side of the horse and ask for halt by correct use of back and legs.

A rider can only be said to have mastered the turn on the hindquarters when he can successfully carry it out at any given place in the school, even in the centre away from the support and help supplied by the wall or track. When he has made this degree of progress, he will have polished his feel to the point at which he can execute correct turns in motion, make his horse flex properly and canter on.

Turns in motion

By this term we mean any change of direction (left, right, half-left, half-right), cornering and riding in circles, small circles and serpentines. A rider will be able to carry out good turns in motion only if he has learned to coordinate his influences and give them the right degree of emphasis when turning at the halt. Most likely,

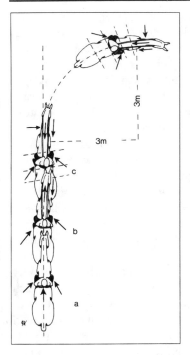

55 Turns in motion. To keep the diagram simpler, the leaning to the inside of the horse when turning (centrifugal force) has been omitted (see p. 44).

during the early stages of his riding lessons, the rider will have been on an obedient horse equipped with side-reins on which to improve his sense of balance, and such a horse will carry out turns without any aid from the rider. But this will suffice to teach the rider that he should displace his weight to the inside when his horse rounds a corner of the school, for otherwise he would experience a tendency to slip off to the outside. Similarly with riding a bicycle, a turn is made more by the displacement of weight than anything else.

Each turn in motion is preceded by a half-halt. This alerts the horse and enables the rider to make any necessary adjustment of his seat. The horse is then made to bend towards the side to which the turn is being made while, simultaneously, the rider shifts his centre of gravity to the inside with his inside leg on the girth and the outside one behind it.

A turning aid as such is not given until the horse has achieved flexion in the appropriate direction. The inside rein shows the horse the turn and is used gently to maintain the bend.

56 A collected trot on the left rein. The horse is flexed a little to the inside; the right (outside) leg prevents the quarters from swinging outwards; the left (inside) leg keeps the momentum in the left hind leg. Dr Josef Neckermann riding Antoinette.

The outside rein and outside leg work as they do in the turn on the hindquarters; in other words, they make the horse deviate from a straight path, control the amount of the curve it describes and prevent its shoulder (forehand) or croup (quarters) moving outwards. The inside leg also increases its driving influence to stimulate the horse's inside hind leg.

Both legs and both reins are used positively but to varying degrees and with different emphases depending on what the rider wants to achieve and the sensitiveness of the horse. If the turn is well executed, the hind feet will follow exactly in the marks made by the fore feet. On a freshly raked track a rider can readily check whether he has made a good turn.

Apart from the influences which the rider seeks to impose, there are other factors which may make the horse go off the track or towards the inside. A horse will tend to cut the corner in the school, and it is therefore necessary for the rider to use his inside leg more strongly to ride the horse well into the corner. Should the horse want to move off the track to the outside, the rider must counter this by using the outside leg and outside rein. It is a useful exercise for the

57 (left) A right turn in the jumping arena. Hans Günter Winkler. The horse is flexed to the right. The rider is influencing in the same way as the rider in illustration 56.

58 (right) Senior Rider Lindenbauer performing a pirouette to the left. The horse is turning on its quarters at a collected canter with a definite bend to the left. The deep rounding of the haunches is obvious. Distinct cadence and an even sequence of steps are necessary in this movement.

59 Split-seconds are all-important in show-jumping. Tight turns call for careful calculation. In this photograph one can see how well engaged the horse's hind legs are. Nelson Pessoa on Gran Geste. (He is influencing in the same way as the rider in illustration 58.)

rider to describe a circle with the quarters to the inside and to the outside alternately, while making sure that the forehand remains on the track. This should only be attempted at the walk and for short periods of time. It is a common fault for riders to think early on that they can manage good turns in motion. It is extremely difficult to ride small circles with the fore hoof-prints and the hind hoof-prints coinciding, demanding as it does just the right amount of emphasis and coordination of the influences. If a

60 Turns in motion.
Left: the inside leg is acting too strongly (a not-too-important fault in rounding the corner of the school).
Right: the outside leg is acting too strongly (a not-too-important fault in turning in the centre of the school).

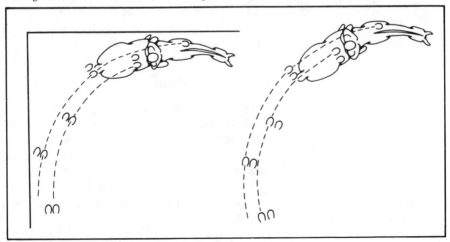

rider thinks he has mastered this, he should put himself to the test of riding one or two small circles on the same track in the same place. This should be done, of course, on a freshly raked school, and he may be shocked by what the hoof-prints indicate. It is a useful aid to the rider trying to develop his sense of feeling for turning if he not only performs these exercises on his own horse but also on unfamiliar horses.

After every turn in motion, the horse must take up a straight position once again. In carrying out circles with changes of rein, the horse must be straight just before reaching the centre of the school where the rein will be changed, and be made to flex in the other direction.

In a change of rein in the circle (see illustration 72, p. 152), the change should be made towards the closed side, not the open side of the circle. The horse must be straightened just before the centre of the circle. It is important to ride the correct school figure, not just because it is called for, but because, if the rider does not take pains to make equal arcs through the circle, he will not give correct aids for the turns. He will only give his horse clear training instructions if he is quite sure of the line he ought to take.

It is equally important in riding serpentines that the horse be made to flex appropriately, with its being straightened before each change of direction. And the rider should ensure that the flexion each time is thorough: in other words, the flexion is in the whole of the horse from poll to tail. Serpentines, then, are extremely good training for both rider and horses.

SHARP HALF-TURNS

A sharp half-turn is a smoothly executed turn in motion on the hindquarters. While the turn on the hindquarters already described is carried out at halt, the sharp half-turn is made at walk and canter. If done at a trot, the horse must be brought briefly to walk, performs the movement smoothly at this pace, then goes on straight away in trot.

Practice should be initially at the walk and

one proceeds in a way similar to that which was employed in practising turns on the hindquarters, bringing the horse to a halt from walk while making it flex as it does so and thereby making the first step of the turn. The aids are identical but care must be taken that impetus is not lost and that the horse continues in the same cadence with both hind legs as at the start of the movement.

Half-circling in motion is a useful preparation for sharp half-turns. A half-circle is ridden with the horse completing it at an angle to the track. At more advanced stages of dressage it is recommended that the rider, in performing these half-circles in motion, narrows them with his outside leg. It is especially useful if this is done at canter. A half-circle at canter ridden in this way is quite the best way to prepare for the sharp half-turn at canter which will later lead to the pirouette (see illustration 59, p. 133).

It is vital not to let one's desire to execute smooth sharp half-turns lead one into the error of hurrying things up by pulling on the reins. The speed with which the horse revolves is not important: what is important is that the horse takes correct steps evenly. Needless to say, horses that are not obedient to the aids will resist such movements and show their unwillingness by head-tossing, taking steps backwards and rearing.

DECREASING AND INCREASING THE CIRCLE

Decreasing and increasing the circle are turns in motion that are aimed at making rider and horse familiar with the influences that are required to reduce or increase the diameter of a circle. The horse moves in a circle in spiral fashion until it is describing a half-circle, then outwards again until it is, once more, circling. It remains, at all times, flexed towards the inside.

When decreasing the circle, the forehand is pushed to the inside by the influence of the outside rein, and the quarters to the inside by the outside leg. The inside rein is used softly and maintains the flexion.

Similarly, when increasing the circle, the outside rein plays the biggest role, while the inside leg pushes the horse gradually to the outside. No attempt must be made to widen the circle by trying to push the horse outwards by taking the inside rein over the horse's withers.

These exercises are not easy for a novice rider and should not be attempted early on. A rider should have acquired a secure, steady seat and should understand the interaction of the influences. A useful way to start them is to ride circles with quarters in or quarters out (see illustration 60, p. 133).

Striking off into canter

The canter is a pace of three beats.[1] One may canter right or canter left. In cantering right, the right-hand pair of legs leads (illustration 62, phase b, in cantering left, the left-hand pair of legs leads. A novice rider is usually allowed to do a little cantering in his first lessons, as it gives him a sense of exhilaration and makes riding more exciting for him, and turning the corners gives him some idea of balance. But, at this early stage, little is said on the correct way to strike off into canter. Most horses will react to the instructor's voice, obeying his raised tone. But the beginner should learn correctly from the very start how to canter off as only then will he sit well and properly in the canter movement. Similarly, we remarked how the beginner should acquire the ability to harmonise his body with the horse's movements in the trot by learning how to brace his back, walk on and halt.

In asking for the canter, in addition to making a half-halt to make the horse listen, it is necessary to make it flex to the right or the left, depending on which lead is intended. The rider should have a definite lead in mind and be sure to give his aid accordingly.

This aid will not be given from an even seat but the seat that the rider took up to make his horse flex to right or left. His inside hip will

[1]One can hear three beats in every canter movement. (The trot has two beats, as has also the rein-back, if correctly executed. The walk has four beats.)

already be slightly forward, his inside leg on the girth and outside leg about a hand's width behind the girth. If the rider now were to push the horse forward using back and legs with equal emphasis while allowing with the reins, the horse would trot on, flexed to the right or to the left.

But since a canter right or canter left is required and not trot, the sequence of steps needs to be altered appropriate to the canter. The main stimulus for this is the very definite pushing forward of the inside seat-bone and the bracing of the back on one side. At the same time, both legs urge the horse forward (inside one on the girth; outside one about a hand's width behind it), with the inside one being most important. Both reins must allow, to permit forward movement, but pressure on the inside rein may be increased by a slight restraint of the outside rein.

The most important influence is that exerted by the back. In advanced dressage this alone will suffice not just to make the horse strike off into canter but also to make it change the lead during the canter. However, as a back aid should not be contemplated without reinforcement from the legs, the transition from strongly executed to refined aids will hardly be perceptible.

Opinions differ on the way to strike off into canter. It can be achieved by use of the whip, with the voice or a click of the tongue. Some maintain the horse should be flexed to the outside to free its shoulders more. This would give it an S shape. Others hold that one should use the outside leg only, but all such advice is invalid.

A rider will achieve a good strike off into canter when he is sitting in complete accord with the horse's movements. There is a simple test of whether one is sitting in this way. If one is unable to tell when the horse is cantering on the wrong lead, one has incontrovertible proof that the seat is inadequate. This point needs elaboration.

A well-trained horse flexes somewhat to the right when cantering right, and left when cantering left. It is not just leading with its inside legs but with its entire muscle structure, including the muscles of its flexed back, in con-

61 Cantering off on the right lead.

a: Influencing with both legs and back, half-halt.

b: Horse is flexed to the right, the right leg is acting on the girth with the left leg supporting behind the girth.

c: Cantering off.

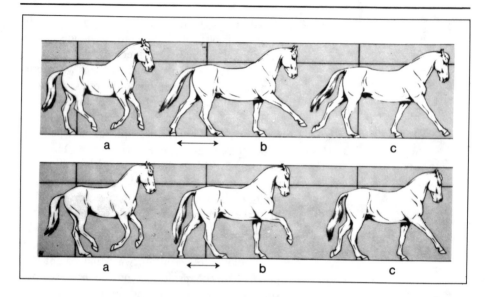

62 Stages in cantering on the right lead.
Top: strong canter. Bottom: collected canter. Letter f denotes the point at which the horse has all four legs off the ground (suspension). The continuous line shown near the top of each illustration is the same height from the track.

formity. For the rider then to accommodate himself to these movements and sit deeply in the saddle as he did at the trot, he must push forward his inside seat-bone and hip by back-muscle action on the appropriate side. When he can manage this he will be totally secure in the saddle just as he was at the trot.

If the rider pushes his inner side forward with the horse cantering on with opposite leg leading, he will be out of harmony with the horse's movement and will not be able to sit properly. He should therefore be able to feel with his seat that the horse is on the wrong lead, for the horse's motion will oppose the way he is trying to sit. While he, let us say, would be trying to push forward his right hip and right seat-bone, the horse's movement would tend to throw forward his left hip and left seat-bone and a twisting effect would be apparent in his buttocks which would prevent a secure seat in the saddle. Once the rider realises the significance of this, his feeling will develop rapidly.

Once the rider has mastered the way to make his horse strike off into canter, he will be able to do so with the right or left leg leading as he chooses and be in a position to instruct his horse properly.

The canter on movement is best performed

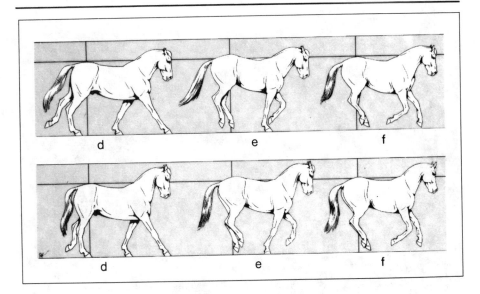

from walk in a small circle or when approaching the corner of the school and this should continue until the rider has achieved a level of skill. One sits properly more easily at walk and a horse, when flexed in a turn, will strike off more readily.

As training progresses, an effort should be made to see that the horse's hindquarters are not flexed too greatly to the inside prior to cantering on and that it keeps to a single track.

The canter

There should not be just 'a canter' but something more specific: working canter, collected canter, medium canter, extended canter. A rider should be aware of the different paces, should try to carry them out properly, and, by changing them frequently, avoid the pitfall of just cantering at an undefined tempo.

One gets a very different feeling in the canter from that which one gets at the trot. The canter is a sort of bounding movement with a different foot-sequence. A rider who has learned to accommodate himself to a trotting movement still has to practise to do this in the canter. Some riders manage the one pace better than the other. A deep, secure seat in the canter is closely bound up with the way in which the canter is initiated

63 Working canter on the left rein with no rein contact or collection. Irmgard von Opel riding Arnim.

64 Natural upright self-carriage with the rider in a forward or half-seat. An English hunter being ridden by a judge.

65 Compare this unnatural carriage of the horse which is undesirable.

and is therefore totally dependent on a good canter on. One cannot over-emphasise the importance of a rider's acquiring an awareness of how the horse moves at this pace.

In the canter, the rider has no choice but to participate in the up-and-down movements made by the forehand and hindquarters. When the horse in the initial first phase is higher in front, the rider tends to lean forward and bring his seat out of the saddle. This is wrong. When the horse in the third phase of the movement is lower in front, the rider leans back a little.[1] The faster a horse canters, the faster its movements of course, but also the longer its strides become. The tighter the turns it is desired to make at this pace, the more collected the canter must be and the more weight the haunches must be prepared to bear. In a collected canter, the quarters are low with the forehand relatively high. One speaks of a 'shortened' canter when a rider erroneously slows the tempo by using the reins

[1] It is instructive to take a photograph of a rider and horse in the second phase of the canter action, when the horse has three legs in contact with the ground. At this instant the rider should be sitting properly, neither leaning forward nor backward. If one watches closely and counts, one can manage to take the photograph at the right moment.

instead of collection. The horse is then cantering not with the desired 'round' outline but by dragging or trailing its quarters, and irregular steps will frequently be a consequence.

At the canter the horse is collected by half-halts, just as it was at trot. This is best practised by the novice rider after he has successfully learned how to achieve collection in the canter by asking frequently for canter on. The first canter stride is invariably the one with the most elevation, but collection starts to be lost with the second or third canter stride. This is because an aid was correctly given to initiate the movement but not maintained in the subsequent canter strides: this keeping up the momentum is something the rider has to remember. He must bear in mind that, just as in the trot where he had to drive with equal back-muscle influence, to carry out half-halts, to collect and sit deeply in the saddle, so must he work in the canter with, additionally, a need to give, at each stride, what amounts to a repeated aid for canter on. As training progresses, such an aid becomes less emphatic until, ultimately, back-muscle pressure on one side is all that is necessary. There are many riders who are capable of sitting well in the trot and whose horses listen to them, but who have never grasped that back-muscle pressure on one side in the canter plays the same role as equal back-muscle pressure in the trot.

Bending and flexing

Bending and flexing are both a necessary part of the horse's training. We shall touch on this subject because, at some time or another, every rider will wonder what this term involves.

Just as physical exercises can loosen our joints and muscles, appropriate exercises can loosen the muscles of a horse and make it supple. These exercises are a useful preparation for lateral work and shoulder-in (see p. 147 and illustration 20, p. 46).

In the case of bending, the horse should bend along its whole length as it would be in moving in a flexed position (see illustrations 67 and 68, pp. 145 and 146), except that the forehand is a

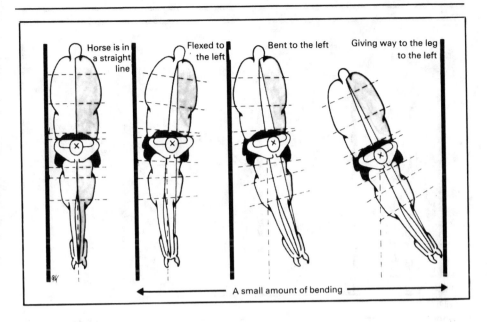

67 Riding in a flexed position on two tracks. When
performing shoulder-in, the horse cannot bend away from the
wall more than is illustrated because he cannot bend any more
in the ribs than this. The outside leg has to be used with extra
emphasis to prevent the quarters from swinging out as they do
in giving way to the leg.

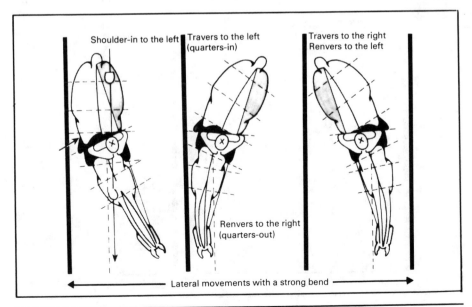

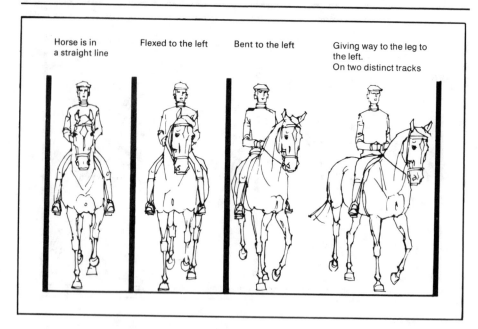

Horse is in a straight line

Flexed to the left

Bent to the left

Giving way to the leg to the left. On two distinct tracks

68 Riding in a flexed position on two tracks. Each rider depicted is moving straight towards the observer. Each appears to be sitting perfectly straight, although slightly inclined to the inside, but with no hint of collapse at the hips. The horses are moving in a flexed position but in a straight line and not sideways. Impulsion and energy have to be maintained otherwise the exercise is pointless.

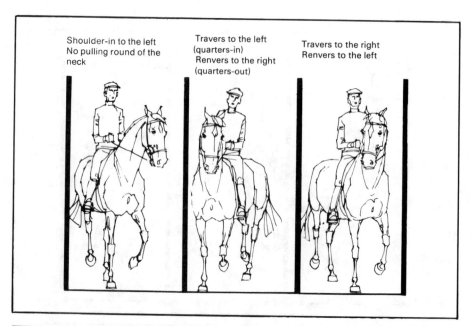

Shoulder-in to the left No pulling round of the neck

Travers to the left (quarters-in) Renvers to the right (quarters-out)

Travers to the right Renvers to the left

Riding on two tracks

In working on a single track, the hind legs follow the track of the forelegs. If the horse moves at an angle to its line of direction, it is said to be on two tracks. However, these two tracks should not diverge to the extent that regular paces or cadence are lost or the rhythm destroyed. A consequence could be damage to legs and tendons.

Exercises on two tracks call for a totally secure seat and much sensitivity, and can therefore have anything but the desired effect if practised by a beginner.

'Giving way to the leg' or 'leg yielding' and 'side movements' are part and parcel of work on two tracks. Giving way to the leg is a suppling exercise, in which two distinct tracks are involved, with the legs stepping over and in front of each other; the horse is at a marked angle to the direction selected with a small amount of bend. Its head is turned away from this direction. Giving way to the leg is not concerned with stimulating the horse's quarters or achieving collection; it is a way of reinforcing the inside aids and is a very useful yardstick by which a rider can evaluate the effectiveness of his forward and sideways driving influences and how they interact with the influences that are supportive or restraining. It should be carried out at walk and only on rare occasions at trot and only for short periods. There is no practical point in trying out giving way to the leg in the corners of the school.

In giving way to the leg the horse moves on two tracks – they may be separated from each other by up to one pace – with its head turned a small amount, and with the inside legs crossing equally in front of and over the outside legs (see illustrations 67 and 69).

The rider should sit with emphasis to the inside and apply sideways pressure to the quarters with his inside leg placed just behind the girth. The pressure should be applied the moment the inside hind leg leaves the ground and be re-applied, if necessary, from step to step. The outside rein keeps the forehand on its part-

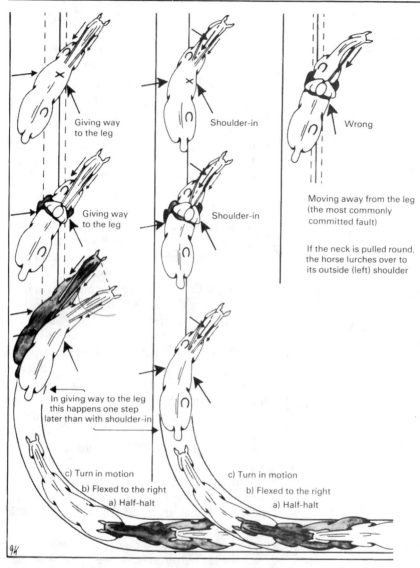

Giving way
to the leg

Shoulder-in

Wrong

Giving way
to the leg

Shoulder-in

Moving away from the leg
(the most commonly
committed fault)

If the neck is pulled round,
the horse lurches over to
its outside (left) shoulder

In giving way to the leg
this happens one step
later than with shoulder-in

c) Turn in motion
b) Flexed to the right
a) Half-halt

c) Turn in motion
b) Flexed to the right
a) Half-halt

69 The procedure for giving way to the leg and shoulder-in when coming out of a corner.

icular track. Any attempt by the horse to get away from the leg and any drawing away of the outside shoulder should be countered by supportive use of the outside leg and outside rein.

By 'side movements' we mean shoulder-in, quarters-in (travers) and quarters-out (renvers). They serve the purpose of completing the gymnastic training of the horse and of increasing its ability to bend along its length (i.e. in the ribs). They should be attempted only by riders whose seat is beyond reproach and who have years of

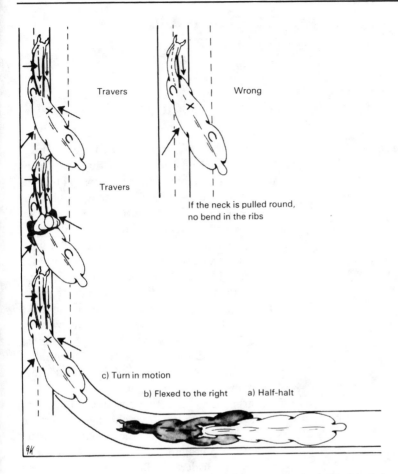

Travers

Wrong

Travers

If the neck is pulled round,
no bend in the ribs

c) Turn in motion

b) Flexed to the right   a) Half-halt

70 The procedure for travers coming
out of a corner.

practice and experience behind them. Side movements are not an end in themselves but are an essential part of the horse's training: by aiming to increase its flexibility they can lead to a greater degree of collection.

In shoulder-in, the inside hind leg follows the same line as the outside foreleg (see illustrations 67 and 68).

In quarters-in and its counterpart, quarters-out, the outside hind leg follows the same line as the inside hind leg. One does not often observe this last point being carried out. Usually the horse's quarters or shoulder slide out of line and it is then free from the collecting influences of its rider. When this happens, the whole exercise becomes pointless or even harmful to the training programme.

CHAPTER FOUR

Further Aspects in the Training of Horse and Rider

Riding in the school

Most riders will be taught in class lessons. This is often criticised on the grounds that one learns far more effectively in private lessons. This is not totally true and it can be shown that class lessons do have certain advantages. Apart from the fact they they will certainly cost less, in class lessons, riders seem to be stimulated to greater enthusiasm in company, and instructors have the opportunity to compare the prowess of their pupils at each stage of tuition. Furthermore, there is ample scope to enable the pupils to make frequent changes of horses, which is vital in giving them an awareness of how different horses react. Riding on one's own is essential in all branches of riding but it will benefit the rider if he knows clearly what he wants to practise. And he should have thought this out well in advance when he does get the opportunity to work on his own. Ideally, the instructor should indicate a programme, but, if this is not forthcoming, the rider should map out his own programme.

When riding alone, a rider can practise or concentrate on any particular point he wants to ask his instructor about and maybe ask him if he can try out, say, a horse that is known to present a particular problem.

Solo riding is especially useful in testing one's abilities in the matter of seat, feel and influence, lessons and aids. It is advisable to start with the simple basics: back influence, walking on, halting and making one's body follow the horse's movements.

The way to improve the ability to give aids and influence on one side only is by practising the turn on the hindquarters, and it is important that this be done occasionally at any random place in the middle of the school. For full mastery, the turn on the hindquarters should be practised at walk and then one should go on to sharp half-turns (see p. 134).

It is also easier to practise cantering on (see p. 136) on one's own, for it is much less practical to strike off into canter, make a half-halt and canter on again in a class lesson. But it is vital to practise this aspect of riding because it develops sensitivity, teaches the rider to be at ease in the canter (i.e. securely in the saddle) and is something he will have to master before he will know infallibly when his horse is cantering correctly.

When the rider has progressed to the stage at which he can strike off into canter without any problems, he can gradually begin to ask more of himself and of his horse. He should now break the habit of stopping the canter after three or four strides, for the horse will get to know the pattern and stop of its own accord. He should canter now for three, now for eight, now for five strides, but always a different number. It is no bad thing to count to oneself the number of strides so as not to fall into the error of routine. Proficiency must also be sought on both reins and, when it is achieved, one should practise striking off into canter alternately on the left and right rein.

Another very beneficial exercise is changing in the circle at canter; just before reaching the centre of the circle, a half-halt should be made followed by flexing to the opposite direction and cantering on once again.

It is, then, recommended that one makes these exercises rather more varied and difficult as a means of polishing sensitivity and influence by going from walk to trot to canter, back to walk, once more to canter and so on. It is possible to bring this to the pitch that, in the course of one single circle, one can strike off into canter four times from walk, and trot on four times from walk, and it is equally useful to do this in a straight line, asking the horse to canter sometimes left and sometimes right.

In all these exercises it is important that one works conscientiously; the programme matters less than the thoroughness with which it is per-

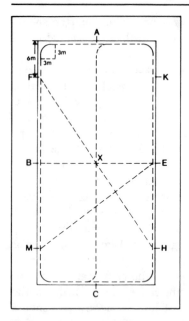

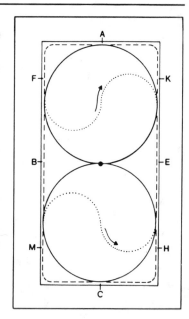

71 Dressage arena 20 metres × 40 metres.

AECBA   whole arena

AEBA   half the arena

AXC   centre line

FXH   line across the whole arena

ME   line across half the arena.

72 Circle lines and change of direction lines.

73 –––serpentine lines on the long side
     . . . .serpentine lines across the arena

74 About-turn. Small circles out of a corner. Figure of eight out of a corner.

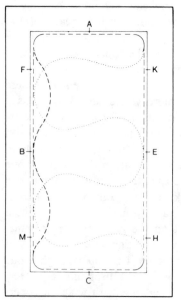

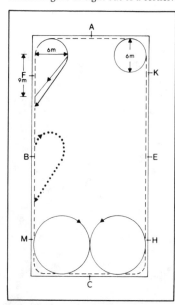

formed. Each exercise must be tackled thoughtfully and be made as clear and straightforward for rider and horse as possible.

Care should be taken when riding alone not to make more than half a circuit of the school without breaking up the pattern with a half-halt or halt, a change of pace or a figure. When all possibilities have been exhausted, it is better to let the horse walk on a long rein and take a rest than to let it meander round the school in a listless state.

School figures

The rider who wishes to perform school figures has to be able to give completely clear aids and the way he carries out these figures shows his instructor how much progress has been made (see pp. 151-153). School figures should not be regarded as an end in themselves but rather as a stage in a particular aim, that of control of the horse. Initially, they will be practised in the school but an early opportunity should be taken to perform them outside so that the rider may learn to cope with extraneous influences which can distract his horse and prevent it concentrating (for example, his horse not wanting to leave its stable or move away from other horses). Outside, the rider will have to deal with situations he will not meet in the school, but which he will have to be prepared for before he takes his horse out across country.

A normal riding school should measure 20 × 40 metres;[1] in other words, the long sides are twice the length of the short ones. From these sides run theoretical connecting lines which divide the area into four symmetrically; this enables the rider to perform figures on both leads. The more progress he makes, the more he will want to practise school figures as a means of refining his aids and developing his horse's obedience.

Of course, school figures are only beneficial when the practitioner seeks to ride them

[1]The dressage arena used in three-day eventing and for certain Medium and Advanced tests measures 20 × 60 metres.

correctly; his success in them will reflect his progress accurately.

Riding out in the countryside

Riding is developed by practice and the greater the enthusiasm a rider has for it, the more enjoyment he will gain from it and the more he will want to put into it. Nothing will accord more with this ideal than riding out in the countryside.

A long hack out, even when there is no one at hand to offer words of correction, will do much for the seat simply because the rider becomes more relaxed. Undulating countryside improves his sense of balance. He invariably sits better than when he is forcing himself to sit in a way that he thinks is correct. And when he has accustomed himself to making long hacks out and has achieved some confidence on his horse, he will not have the same tendency to stiffen up when he is given instruction.

One may say, then, that riding out for novices at an early stage is of more benefit for general riding training than is usually realised. It is in no way a waste of time, as is often asserted. A long steady canter and a long steady trot do an enormous amount for confidence and when, during riding out, something happens to a rider that is outside the area of his experience and with which he cannot cope, he is all the more eager to assail his instructor afterwards with demands for explanation or advice and will look forward to subsequent lessons in the school with extra anticipation.

This apart, hacking out should be regarded as an especially useful training supplement at all stages of a rider's development. A rider who thinks he has good control of his horse indoors should test himself in similar movements outdoors: he may well find things very different away from the peace and quiet of the covered area. It is very obvious outside when a rider sits badly and when he has *really* learned to ride, and what may have seemed adequate indoors is revealed as something assumed rather than truly learned. There, too, it is immediately apparent

75 and **76** Smiling when jumping in
... beaming when jumping out!
Lucinda Prior-Palmer, the British
European Champion, on Village
Gossip masters the difficult water
obstacle at Luhmühlen in 1977.

whether the horse listens properly to the aids and
obeys the rider or whether lip service only has
been paid to the fundamentals. Riding across
country is indubitably the best test of dressage
skills.

The accusation is often made that horses that
have been well schooled indoors go badly across
country and, while this does happen, one should
not condemn training methods on that account.
Certainly, horses that do no school work tend to
go better outside, going more quietly and shying
less, than those who are worked intensively
indoors. But this argument is not really valid. If
school training has been carried out properly,
the horse *will* go anywhere calmly and easily for
its rider. Riding across country is not just a cri-
terion, it is the goal of all dressage. And for this
reason it is absolutely necessary that the horse
does not just give the appearance of listening to
the aids, but is totally obedient to them and that
the rider develops sensitivity to the point at
which he knows when his horse is fully responsive. If these cannot be achieved, then riding out
makes more problems than it solves for both
rider and horse.

POSITION OUT OF THE SADDLE (THE 'LIGHT' SEAT)

When riding across country, one often adopts a position out of the saddle. This must not be confused with the forward seat (see illustration 16, p. 41). In this, the rider's stirrup leathers are of normal length but he leans forward slightly, closing his thighs against the horse a little, while, in the position out of the saddle, he rides two to four holes shorter. It is also necessary that he is in a position to make good knee contact, since his seat will largely be out of the saddle and will thus form no sort of support point for him.

The position out of the saddle is used when cantering, particularly over undulating terrain, when ascending steeply and when jumping. Depending on the activity, the upper body is inclined forward to a varying degree and the seat displaced to the rear correspondingly (to preserve equilibrium). The rider's centre of gravity is thus kept in accord with that of the horse. When accelerating, as, for example, when taking off to clear an obstacle, the rider displaces his centre of gravity forward, and similarly, on landing, he brings it somewhat to the rear. The hip and knee joints are important pivotal points as they have to provide a supple and effective foundation for this kind of 'seat'.

Back influences are transmitted through the thighs to the knees with the upper body straightening slightly and the seat making light contact with the saddle. Coming back to the saddle heavily, as tends to be done on occasion when urging a horse towards an obstacle, is not just unsightly but shows that the rider has not mastered the art of influencing from this riding position. It is a sad fact that one sees such deficiencies all too often in sporting events at a high level, for good style tends to be subordinated to a desire for success. Hands too high, long reins brought right into the body, noisy legs and bent backs; all these are far too much in evidence. The distinguishing features for the position out of the saddle (the 'light' seat) should be borne

77 Horst Karsten rides Sioux across country. He is in the 'light' seat, concentrating on looking well ahead.

78 Richard Meade riding Bleak Hills.

well in mind: low hands, low elbows, low shoulders, low hips (but with the seat out of the saddle), low knees (even though the stirrups are short), heels down, back straight, with the rider looking straight ahead.

The rider should try to lower all his joints – from his shoulders right down to his heels – so as to stay with the horse's centre of gravity: by doing so, he will be in supple harmony with all his horse's movements and be in a position to act directly and decisively whenever it may be necessary.

RIDING UPHILL AND DOWNHILL

Being naturally timid creatures, horses go with great care over uneven ground and cope much better when they are left very much to their own devices. They are rather more skilful in descending than ascending which, in practical terms, means that they can go down much steeper slopes than they can ascend.

Horses will invariably go down the steeper slopes at a walk, and, when the angle of descent exceeds fifty degrees, they tuck their hindlegs neatly under them and slide down on their haunches.

When riding downhill, it is essential that the rider looks ahead to pick a path and does not leave it to chance, with blinkered eyes, as it were. He will have to sit inclined well forward and keep himself from sliding or falling forward by supporting his hands on the horse's withers. From this position he can direct his horse to avoid stones, tree roots and slippery places and pick the best line of descent. In this way he can safely negotiate quite steep descents and, sitting as we have described, he can keep his legs in contact with the horse ready to prevent the quarters from moving to one side or the other, something that must be avoided at all costs. If the horse's hindquarters should move sideways, particularly where it is slippery, say on wet grass, over rocks or in soft sand, it loses its footing and will come down.

A rider who leans back when descending will

For a correct understanding of what is involved in these elements it is necessary to be as consciously aware of the horse's psychology as was suggested in considering what was required in the approach to dressage. It may often appear to the onlooker that a skilful show-jumper works his horses all according to the same pattern. But jumping horses vary like any others: they may be eager or lazy, impetuous or phlegmatic, timid or courageous; one horse will respond to being petted, while another learns more quickly by being punished; some jump more readily and with greater interest than others; this one is a little spoiled, that one much more so.

As always, the horse's capacity for remembering plays a most significant role. It never quite forgets a fall or an obstacle that may have caused it pain; and the horse's temperament will decide whether at the next jump it tucks its legs up a little more carefully or loses its nerve.

One must take note of the smallest details when teaching a horse to jump. Painstaking education is everything in jumping and its importance cannot be over-emphasised. The horse should be schooled in a calm and deliberate manner, quite without haste. The demands one makes on the horse should be increased only gradually and care must be taken that it is not over-taxed: it should be petted and praised, and a lesson should always be brought to an end after it has made a well-executed jump.

In schooling a horse for jumping, one should use solid material for jumps, such as paddock rails and removable walls, etc., rather than brushwood fences which a horse may go round or crash through. A simple rail without a take-off pole in front of it is quite the most difficult obstacle for a horse to get its approach right.

Schooling may be carried out in varying ways and the height of the jumps is immaterial. The procedure to be followed in training a horse to jump 2 metres is no different from that followed in training him to jump 60 cms stylishly; what will be different is that, in the case of the higher jumps, the rider's failings will be much more in evidence, but that is not to say that he will not have these failings in making 60-cm jumps, and they will mar his performance to the same degree.

A rider can commit many faults that make a horse anxious about jumping, but he has very many fewer ways to restore it to keenness. If a rider has made his horse anxious, it is essential to start again by going back to low obstacles. It is impossible to make the horse enthusiastic about jumping by force.

A novice rider is recommended to jump his horse in the direction of the door of the school, towards its stable or towards other horses, but *never* away from its stable or away from other horses.

Training should follow a systematic programme of exercises. One can ask for ten jumps a day, even twenty, as long as they are not too high, but it is necessary not to overdo any other schooling exercises on the same day, as this could all amount to an over-taxing of the horse's strength. Care should be taken to vary the height of the jumps constantly, as this gives the horse practice in estimating its take-off strides.

Jumping schooling may be carried out either in hand or mounted. Both methods tend to be used together. The term 'in hand' is used when the horse jumps without a rider, but this method varies in that the horse may jump quite freely on its own, may be led to the jump, or make the jump on the lunge.

Care should be taken that the reins are well knotted so that the horse cannot put its legs through them. When leading the horse, one does so between the horse and the wall of the school, i.e. if on the right rein to the horse's left, and on the left rein to its right; this is to avoid being kicked.

When jumping a single obstacle one should let the horse make its approach to it only when it is pointing straight at it. One should avoid allowing the horse to round a corner and storm off at a jump; it may lose its footing and it is not a good way to inculcate jumping skills, although it is quite a commonly committed error.

When the horse jumps on the lunge, care must

be taken that the lunge accompanies the movement properly to avoid the horse getting a jab in the mouth as a reward for its efforts.

Sometimes a rider will want to make a single jump or several, one after another. This does not have to take place only in the school but may be practised outside. To do this, one arranges a jumping area in one of three shapes – rectangular, straight or circular. The horse may be asked to make as few or as many jumps as is desired and the distance between jumps can be varied.

Spirited horses get more excited than average school horses. A way to calm a horse is to reduce the height of a jump or ask it to make several jumps positioned closely together, although this second remedy can have the opposite effect to what is intended.

There is simply not one universal formula. One should vary the procedure in conformity with the degree of training and temperament of the horse so as to increase its keenness to jump and to make it consciously work out its approach and take-off strides. A rigidly prescribed method of training would only be detrimental.

Just as much care must be taken in training a horse to jump when mounted. A beneficial and varied way of approaching jumping training is to combine both jumping with and without a rider. Or one may choose to jump for several days or weeks with a rider and then for a similar period of time without one.

Much of the training method will be dictated by where one does one's riding. If at an establishment in or near a town, one will tend to practise mainly in a school. If in rural surroundings, jumping will be practised more outside. But it is essential that the rider tries to fathom out his horse's attitude to jumping and shapes the schooling accordingly. If this is not done, and if he simply believes that all horses may be treated in the same manner, he is unlikely to achieve good results.

APPROACHING A JUMP

The most common error in jumping is that insufficient care is taken in the approach. It is the take-off that decides the execution of a jump. There is an old saying: 'Throw your heart over a jump and go on after it!' A horse feels what is in its rider's mind through his influences and how definite they are and is very well aware whether the rider is determined about jumping or is uncertain and apprehensive. If the horse is ridden strongly forward straight at the middle of the jump, it will jump willingly and well. If not, it gets lost and falters and, if it is held back half-heartedly, will stop or run out.

Before jumping, the stirrup leathers should be shortened by two or three holes. The best pace for clearing an obstacle is canter, as the horse is happiest at that pace. It is, of course, possible to jump from walk or trot but canter is the most natural, for the sequence of steps in jumping corresponds to the sequence in canter. When a horse jumps from walk or trot, it has to change the pattern of steps at the last moment. On the right rein one jumps from a canter right and, on the left rein, from a canter left. But some horses will always change the lead just before the jump because they prefer to jump with one particular leg leading. In the case of low jumps, most horses will jump on either lead.

The horse will choose its own speed for the last few take-off strides. In this, it does what an athlete does who is about to make a long or high jump; not to let others tell him what to do about his approach, his speed or his length of stride. If others decided these factors, he would be confused and not be able to jump as well, as high and far, as when the decisions were left to him.

It is very important that a novice rider bears this point in mind, especially one who likes to hold his horse back at the approach strides or tries to urge it on by use of spurs and forceful driving. Some horses like to jump at a relatively slow pace, stretching the neck well forward as if to sniff the jump before going over it, while others like to throw themselves at a jump, accelerating all the time they approach it. These differences in approach are habits that horses almost certainly acquire in the early jumping schooling. It might very well be that the horse who prefers a slow jump would do better to jump at speed and the other way round, but this is something about which it is difficult to be dogmatic and, anyway, making such changes will not be accomplished without the devotion of a great deal of time, and certainly not by an inexperienced rider. As training continues, a horse will improve its approach technique of its own accord. Horses that are well-versed in jumping will usually take high jumps at a collected canter and the longer jumps and open ditches at a brisker pace. Less experienced horses do not make this distinction.

It is totally wrong to try to tell a horse when to take off by pulling the reins, by lifting it with the reins, or by using the whip or voice. One notices experienced riders managing this sometimes for some reason of their own, but these are exceptions and not to be followed. A shout can do nothing for a novice rider except, perhaps, to give him courage.

A great deal of serious practice is required before one can use the whip properly. It is almost impossible to avoid shifting the seat slightly in doing so and thus disturbing the horse. It is difficult enough to follow the horse's movement fully over a jump and the difficulties are compounded if one has to take the reins in one hand while keeping them still and administer a tap with the whip in the other hand.

If a horse swerves aside from an obstacle or makes a stop, there can be numerous reasons for its doing so: it may have been insufficiently prepared for the kind of obstacle that it is faced with or its training has not developed far enough; perhaps it has not met, for example, a ditch before or may fear a particular obstacle because it had a fall previously.

Then again, if the rider's heart is not in clearing the obstacle, or his reins, legs, weight or whip are badly used, the horse will be effectively inhi-

83
82
87
86

88

80-88 (From right to left) A good example of masterly riding. Eddie Macken, the Irishman, coping with the Derby Bank/Fence combination at the Derbyplatz in Hamburg-Klein Flottbeck.

81

80

85

84

bited. It may not like the kind of obstacle or take exception to the way it looks. Extraneous noises and similar distractions can provide disturbing factors, as can the presence of other horses nearby.

Clearly, the nature of the refusal dictates the remedy to be applied. There can be no universal panacea for faults arising from such different sources. We cannot, therefore, offer a single universally valid remedy within the framework of this book. Sometimes one needs to tidy up the approach to an obstacle, to adjust the obstacle itself, even check one's tack, possibly put aside the whip and ride with greater conviction. Very often, it will suffice simply to turn the horse and ride at the obstacle once again. It may help to rein back a few paces. Should a longer approach be necessary (and the value of this is inevitably over-estimated), it is suggested that one reins back for several paces and then makes a turn. As a general rule, when it is impossible to pinpoint the reason for a horse refusing, the fault lies solely in the rider's lack of boldness. A rider should have enough self-awareness and honesty to admit this. If the same horse with a different rider does jump an obstacle cleanly, then, of course, one has unmistakable proof of such a fact.

Above all, a rider should remain calm if he does get refusals from his horse and not vent his anger blindly on the horse, who is, in all probability, totally blameless in the matter.

THE RIDER'S POSITION DURING THE JUMP

In a discussion on jumping, most people think the important thing is the rider's seat during the jump. But it cannot be over-emphasised that, while this is of importance, it is not so to the extent that is commonly assumed. Schooling the horse to jump and the approach are certainly as significant. After all, a clumsy beginner will not cut too bad a figure on a horse well-versed in jumping. But, in the long run, if one were to ride a good jumper over obstacles in a listless and apathetic manner, the horse would soon lose its enthusiasm for jumping. We see from photographs that many very successful jumping riders have by no means a perfect seat, but their horses jump keenly and well for them. The other side of the coin is that the best style in the world will not help if the rider lacks nerve and does not know how to attack a jump.

A rider is considered to be sitting in harmony when jumping with his horse when his centre of gravity and that of his horse are in accord: they are then in equilibrium.

In the first phase of the jump, just after the take-off, certain factors affect decisively the rider's ability to follow the horse's movements:

a the sudden acceleration,
b the change of direction from horizontal to upwards.

The steeper the jump, the greater will be the angle upwards. That does not mean the higher the obstacle, but the horse's trajectory upwards, and this depends on whether he takes off standing well away from the obstacle or near it.

For the rider to remain in harmony with his horse, he has to bring his centre of gravity in front of that of his horse; this means that he has to abandon his vertical seat and lean well forward, with the result that, in a high jump, his seat is out of the saddle. The slower the pace of the approach, the less this will happen.

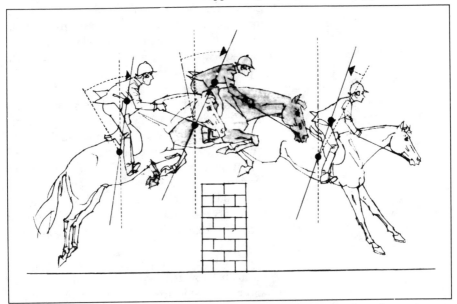

89 The correct seat over a jump. The various lines link the changing centres of gravity of horse and rider and illustrate the adjustments of position the latter has to make to stay in harmony with the former's movements. These could not be deduced from the simple leaning-forward of the rider's body.

In the second phase, the horse's movement upwards ceases and he is travelling forward, horizontally over the obstacle. Even though the rider's centre of gravity is still in front of the horse's, it will not be so far in front of the perpendicular through the horse's back as it was just previously. At this stage, the rider could bring his seat back down to the saddle, but does not do so because it is important not to place a load on the horse's back while the jump is in progress.

In the third phase, before landing, the rider's centre of gravity is still in front of the horse's and would still be so even if he were to sit perpendicular to the horse's back.

Before the jump, a rider is not going to know just how his horse will jump. He must therefore always be prepared to raise his seat and must try to gain experience in gauging to what extent he must bring forward his centre of gravity. In this connection it can be of great help to study photographs, but one should not lose sight of the fact that what is vital is the relative positions of the two centres of gravity.

Moreover, one should not fall into the error of thinking that inclining the upper body forward is necessarily the same as bringing the centre of gravity forward. It would not be difficult, when inclining the upper body forward, to push the seat to a position behind the saddle; one would then be sitting, as on a motorcycle, with the centre of gravity somewhat to the rear, and this is a fault that can often be observed.

Once a rider has grasped the essentials of the jumping seat, he need worry no longer about whether his seat should be in the saddle or not. The problem resolves itself in a very simple way. If one gets one's centre of gravity sufficiently forward with one's seat in the saddle, all well and good. If, though, in order to bring the centre of gravity sufficiently forward, one has to raise the seat from the saddle, again, all well and good.

Now, a rider will need to replace the support normally provided by his seat in the saddle by another equally firm one, and this is so important a point that it is impossible to over-emphasise it. This new support is principally a firm gripping with the knees. The knees must be in the closest possible contact with the horse's body as if they were screwed there. Even if a stirrup leather should give way, the rider should not lose his position immediately.

For the jumping position, the stirrup length should be shorter, as this raises the knees and facilitates a firmer contact, the feet are further forward in the irons – up to the instep – but the heels must not be raised. The legs retain a position just behind the girth. It would be wrong to bring them further back or take them away from the horse's sides. The horse would find either of these an irritation. The reins are somewhat shorter, with the hands resting on either side of the horse's neck. The arms are bent as usual so that the rider can give with the whole arm if it should be necessary.

The horse takes off into the jump from the canter stride (see illustration 62) in which it pushes off from the ground with its forelegs and then, getting its hind legs well underneath its body, projects itself over the obstacle. This point marks the beginning of the rise and is effectively the last moment the rider can make a conscious effort to displace his weight forward. The earlier he has prepared himself for this, the easier he will find things at the moment of rising.

If it becomes necessary to drive the horse forward, one will be obliged to sit until just before the take-off; the effective driving influence of the seat will cease immediately the rider's seat leaves the saddle. Even skilled riders may well find on occasion, despite their experience, that, if it has been necessary to drive their horse right up to an obstacle, they are too late in their action to bring the weight of the body forward and are then behind the movement. Should this happen, no extension of the arms or leaning forward in the saddle will accomplish anything. These attempts to rectify a fault will appear very obvious to an onlooker and may appear to him to be overdone but they are simple manifestations that the rider has lost touch with his horse, is out of phase with him and that he is no longer in a state of equilibrium. What is more, if the rider does not tighten his grip with knees and legs, the horse will probably shoot forward from between his legs. A rider who finds himself behind the movement in this way owes it to his horse at the very least not to increase further the horse's problems by holding on to the reins and not to reward its efforts over the jump by crashing down on its back on landing.

A horse that has good jumping schooling will approach an obstacle readily and, on such a horse, a rider can take up a jumping position much earlier. In fact, if one wants to take several successive jumps on a horse that goes forward freely, it is best to retain this position until the jumps have been completed. In this case, one will drive with the legs only.

In jumping, the rider's hands are low on the horse's neck and this, coupled with the fact that the reins are shorter, gives him a definite contact with the horse's mouth and he can take any appropriate action quickly. However, such a contact is light – one is thinking in terms of only a feather-light contact – and therefore it is of no great account if it is relinquished at the moment of take-off and the reins hang loosely. What would be very wrong would be to take up a strong contact and then incommode the horse by a tug in the mouth. A rider must picture to himself the shape his horse will want to take up over a jump and allow it to stretch its neck and go on freely. With an extended neck, the horse will jump more happily and safely. If, during a jump, a rider feels a stronger contact with the horse, then this is a certain indication that he has committed some fault.

A novice rider can best acquire the jumping seat by riding a well-trained horse without reins, holding the horse's mane or a neck strap. It would not do to hold on to the pommel of the saddle because this will not help the problem of being left behind the movement and makes one totally unable to follow it.

When a rider gets to the point at which he can accommodate himself to the horse's movement over a jump, he will soon progress to the stage at which he can retain balance by supporting his hands on the horse's neck and does not need to hold on to the mane or a strap. This is the time, too, for the novice rider to test his progress by jumping without stirrups to evaluate his ability to grip with his knees. Jumping with the body in a particular position, for example with arms crossed, serves no purpose at all and will only encourage the rider to remain behind the movement.

MISTAKES THE HORSE MAY MAKE IN JUMPING

From time to time even the best jumping horse may make a mistake in a jump and:

1 get too near the obstacle and be obliged to take off very steeply,
2 take off too soon and have to stretch itself over the jump,
3 underestimate the height of the obstacle and have to throw the quarters sideways to avoid hitting it.

At these times it is essential that the rider be able to help his horse and not make life difficult for it with the reins. Therefore a jump should invariably be made with the arms bent at the elbows to facilitate a possible lengthening of them, for the horse needs to achieve balance with its neck in all these movements. If, at the crucial moment – and we are talking of mere fractions of a second – the horse cannot stretch freely, its ability to rectify faults is diminished and, depending on the circumstances, considerable problems may arise.

90 Letting the hands go forward allows the horse to balance itself by stretching to the maximum its head and back; however, a soft contact with the horse's mouth is retained. Major Kurd Albrecht von Ziegner riding Alpenmärchen.

91 Boldness over the triple bars. Rider and horse are in perfect accord. Mary Chapot (USA) on Vestryman.

PECKING

Rein contact is not essential in landing after a jump even if the horse lands clumsily. Here, a contact only slightly too strong could have dire consequences. Many falls on landing occur simply through the rider trying to be helpful.

A novice may think he can lift his horse in front by using the reins but he inevitably pushes it down behind. By a pull at the mouth or an over-strong rein contact, many a rider has deprived his horse of a last-ditch recovery. In just the same way, a tightrope-walker who is off-balance will fall if his balancing pole catches some obstruction at the crucial moment. A horse can only succeed in extricating itself from the consequences of pecking by using its neck and head.

The rider is best advised to sit stockstill and be as calm and firm in the saddle as possible, avoiding any shifting of his weight that might cause his horse to fall. It must be remembered that a rider is a solid body (not a balloon with a lifting power) who, as such, must remain as one with his horse. It is the rider with the most secure seat who will cope best with a peck.

92 The rider is well behind the
movement, has no leg contact, is
hanging on with the reins and is
making jumping most difficult for his
horse.

93 This rider is also behind the
movement but he, at least, is allowing
his horse to use its neck freely and
make a safe landing. Sepp von
Radowitz riding Monte Rosa.

Nor should a rider make the assumption when his horse pecks and takes a stronger pull that the horse has sought such a contact and that it has helped him. After all, a man with tied hands would try to flail about with his hands if he were about to fall down.

LANDING

On landing, a rider's knees are to some extent shock absorbers; they have elasticity and make life easier for the horse as they are not part and parcel of the horse's body but only press against it by the rider's muscles. Likewise, the arms which are supported on the hands have a built-in sprung effect provided by elbow and shoulder joints. The seat, which at the take-off and during the jump has been concerned to relieve the horse's back of weight, comes back to the saddle but without actually settling into it until the horse's hind legs are once more on the ground. The body remains inclined slightly forward.

The rider must resume full control as soon as possible after completion of the jump and be able to influence fully so that he can tell his horse with total mastery whether to go straight on,

94 (left) A high jump beautifully executed. Perfection! If the rider had remained in the saddle he would have been hopelessly behind the movement. E. V. Campion riding Garrai Eoin.

95 (right) Jumping down from a bank. It is easier to go with the horse's movement when jumping downwards than when taking a high jump. One can also easily see if a rider tackles it courageously. Note here the good straight line between elbows and horse's mouth and the relatively loose martingale. Hans Günter Winkler on Halla.

whether to turn, or whether to jump a new obstacle. He must rectify his seat and adjust his feet in the stirrups as may be necessary and take up a proper rein contact.

Special attention must be paid to landing after a high jump. If there is a steep drop, and particularly when jumping into water, which, depending on its depth, will tend to slow the horse to a greater or lesser extent, the rider must take care to displace the weight of his body to the rear in order to relieve the horse's forehand. This will enable the horse to balance itself better on landing and will put its rider in a better position to sit more securely if an unexpected peck occurs.

Riding in competitions

The criticism is often made that riding in competitions is bad for the character, since riding is no longer a goal in its own right but is pushed into the background by ambition and rivalry. Nevertheless, training for competitive work is of special significance, for ambition is the most powerful stimulus to man, spurring him on to undreamt-of achievements, feeding his power of application and endurance and making him ponder and evaluate.

Jumping and cross-country competitions demand additionally from a rider qualities of courage and will-power which he can transmit to his horse. Riding is generally held to be of great educational value to the young and it is no bad thing for youth to be asked to display ability and character in public. It gives pleasure to be awarded the victor's rosette and it is equally necessary to be able to lose with dignity.

For anyone who takes part in competitions, it is important that both rider and horse work together in a lower category and master the requirements for this category before trying to progress to a higher one. If this is not observed, the rider may well cut a sorry picture (which will not do much for his standing or that of his instructor) and his horse will be affected in ways that may take much time and patience to rectify.

It gives an onlooker much more pleasure to see a well-executed Preliminary dressage test than a painfully executed Advanced test. And this inevitably happens when a rider overestimates his capabilities. The same advice applies to show-jumping and cross-country competitions. Riders and horses must make their way into the higher classes only after intensive work and perhaps years of application. There is no other way of achieving that perfect harmony. Any attempt to hasten work is counter-productive and will lead to failure in the long term.

HUNTING

No other aspect of riding does more to show it at its aesthetic best than hunting. No one who has ridden a keen horse behind a lively pack of hounds ever gets the thrill out of his system as long as he lives. In the hunting field the rider will feel that everything comes together. As he gallops briskly through meadows and fields, through valleys and woods, up hills and over ditches, over walls and fences, when his pulse races with the excitement of the chase, he will understand the true significance of his long wearisome hours spent in the riding school. From very early times hunting has been considered the prince of sporting activities and has kept its exclusive character through centuries. It knows nothing of competition and records and therefore there is nothing in it that gives rise to jealousy and ill-will or the desire to secure advantages. It is truly a gentleman's sport. To take part in it calls for nerve and courage, the ability to control one's horse, and, last but not least, it benefits horse-breeding since it requires good hunting horses.

It is not necessary for the horse to be able to catch the eye of a judge in the show ring or that it be young and good looking. Hunting is an extreme test of performance in which temperament plays at least as big a part as physical conformation. The horse must go well across country and not refuse at a ditch or fence, it should not stumble or need pushing; above all, it should not lean on the bit. In the hunting field all horses go with more enthusiasm than they normally show. Many a horse who has been considered lazy and sluggish comes suddenly to life in this sort of company and is hard to hold. On the other hand, it is no great treat to hurtle through the rest of the hunt on a horse that there is no holding; this is a danger both to oneself and to others. It needs experience to choose a hunter and a young rider is well advised to take counsel on this.

Things happen quickly when hunting, and, if a rider lacks experience and that calmness that comes with experience, he will not control his horse properly by correct influences and half-halts; he will, at best, go along as well as he can, steering his horse in the right direction. The more deliberately the horse goes, the better the rider's chances of familiarising himself with the tempo of a hunt.

Before the meet starts, one should check the tack including martingale if fitted (see p. 185) and above all verify that the bandages are secure (see p. 188). A riding stick is best left at home. Stirrup length should be two holes shorter than normal. Experienced riders adopt a jumping position for most of the hunt, supporting themselves not on their seat, but rather in their knees and stirrip-irons. This is much less tiring, especially if the hunt is an arduous one. If, in a long, fast gallop, one is sitting in the saddle, fatigue sets in and it is then difficult to stay with the horse's movements. The tendency then is to get behind the movement and hang on to the reins in both galloping and jumping, with the inevitable interfering with and unbalancing of the horse.

During the hunt a rider should keep his eyes firmly to the front like a motorist; the tempo is faster than usual and it would never do to let oneself be surprised by objects and obstacles that suddenly appear. If one sees another rider in boggy ground or among rabbit holes, one should be able to take action in good time. For this reason one should not ride close behind the person in front so that a view to the front is clear and one is not impeded by any sudden movement his horse may make. Crossing the path of other horses should be avoided and one should keep a straight line: in fact one should try to finish the hunt in the same order as one started off. It makes life difficult for other riders if one goes past them.

A particular point to watch is that, if one's horse refuses at an obstacle, one does not get in the way of those following by turning and obstructing the passage to the obstacle in repeated attempts to clear it. The advice is to follow another horse over the jump but to one side, not right behind it. If the horse still doesn't like the idea (if its fear is stronger than its herd instinct), one should try to go round a ditch or find a narrower part of it, or try to go round a high jump in order to keep contact with the rest of the field. It is especially depressing for a beginner to be far away from the kill. With a modicum of patience and experience he will realise that this can happen even to veteran riders. The better the horse, the easier becomes the whole business of hunting. There is absolutely nothing to be gained by seeking out an obstacle at its highest or widest point: it makes far more sense to look for the easiest way and one does this by looking well ahead. The ambition should be to be in at the kill on a horse that still looks keen and fresh.

If one finds one cannot control the horse, it is advisable to make a way to the side of the field and away from it so as not to impede the progress of others or ride into the hounds (see p. 88 — on how to control a horse that bolts).

No one who has the opportunity of taking part in a hunt should fail to do so. It is essential to have a reasonably decent seat, courage and a good hunter. Every hunt should be an unadulterated joy in a rider's life.

CHAPTER FIVE

Equipment
for Rider and Horse

Equipment for the rider

The clothing worn for riding should bear a relationship to the requirements of the moment. For ordinary riding purposes one puts on what is comfortable and convenient without going to outrageous lengths. However, if appearances are to be made in public events, on festive occasions or in competitions, dress appropriate to the nature of the occasion is necessary. It is not in the terms of reference of this book to go into detail on these matters and any riding instructor can advise on what is correct and what should be avoided.

A black or navy velvet riding hat is normal headwear, while a stiff bowler or top hat is worn in the more advanced dressage circles. In hunting and cross-country riding, the riding hat should be made more secure with a chin support and harness, while a crash helmet is prescribed for cross-country competitions.

THE WHIP

The dressage or schooling whip should be as flexible as possible and weighty at the thick end so that its centre of gravity lies in the user's hand. Given these conditions, it can be flicked well from the hand and no great amount of hand movement need be used to make it effective, unlike the efforts that have to be made when using a riding stick or short whip.

The whip is applied close behind the girth with a definite short tap but the horse should not be startled by any noise made by swishing the whip. When it is necessary to use the whip, it should be applied with appropriate strength and with no hint of uncertainty or tentativeness; the horse must not be in any doubt as to the rider's action. Anger should never be a reason for hitting the horse and one should always be aware of the amount of force one puts into a stroke of the whip.

When mounting, the whip is held in the left hand, but care should be taken that the horse cannot see it, otherwise it may be apprehensive to start off with. Similarly, if a rider already mounted asks another person to hand him a whip, this should be done in such a way that the horse is unaware of it, otherwise it may seek to shy away from it.

The whip is useful as a reinforcement of leg and back influence (see p. 82) when one is riding an untrained horse, when a horse leans on the bit (see p. 85), when a horse fails to respond adequately to leg pressure (as in the case of the unschooled horse, p. 82), when laziness is evidenced or as a punishment.

If a horse does not respond to leg pressure or does so insufficiently, it can be reminded of what is wanted by an immediate small tap of the whip. Such a tap is useful in reinforcing any sideways-driving influence that one is imparting with the leg. Once again, a quick tap applied simultaneously with leg action is all that is called for. If, though, the tap with the whip is delayed and not delivered until after an unsuccessful leg aid, the horse will not be able to understand why the whip was administered; it will not connect the whip with its refusal to carry out the command, will think it is pointless punishment, become apprehensive and its schooling will suffer.

A long whip is unsuitable in cross-country riding or jumping, and, if one needs to carry one, a short whip of no more than 60 to 80 cms length is recommended.

SPURS

A novice rider should not be allowed spurs until he is in full control of his legs. Until he has achieved this he will only succeed in hurting or tickling his horse, who by hopping about will probably bring the rider out of the saddle. But once a rider is sure of his seat and has reasonable control of his lower limbs, he may use spurs. They should be used precisely at the moment when the legs are required to exert a little more emphasis. Over-use of them will lead inevitably to the horse becoming dulled and ignoring them. The less they are used the better. A horse may react against spurs by kicking out with its hind legs and this is usually an indication that the spurs were applied with the wrong amount of pressure, were too hesitantly applied or for too long a period of time. A horse should never object to a swift, decisive touch with the spurs delivered when its attention is to be brought to a certain command. If, in fact, the horse does kick out, the rider should take this as an indication that he is not using his spurs properly. This applies equally when a horse swishes its tail and many horses continue to do this if spurs tickle them. Many riders, when their instructor points out that their horse is showing objection, reply that they are not touching the horse with their spurs: the fact is that they are simply not aware when the spurs are in contact. If a rider does not have this degree of awareness, he should remove the spurs and take pains to rectify this.

To use the spurs, the knee is bent very slightly and calf-pressure is increased. The toes will turn just a little more to the outside. The whole point of using spurs is that they be used exactly at the same moment as the rider employs back and leg influences, otherwise they are useless.

Finally, one should be cautious in using them on ticklish horses and mares in season.

The horse's tack

SADDLES AND BRIDLES

A rider can only sit properly and give correct influences from a well-fitting saddle. The lowest part of this should be at its centre; if it is too far back or too far forward, the rider's seat will be adversely affected. If the lowest point of the saddle is found to be in the wrong place, the reason will be that the channel of the saddle is too long or too narrow, is too high at the rear or is insufficiently padded. A saddle should fit a horse's back as well as a suit fits a man (see illustration 40a, p. 106).

Attention should also be paid to the numnah. When in place under the saddle it should not be wrinkled or folded, which could transmit harmful pressure from the saddle in particular places. Similarly, the girth should be positioned with care and not be nearer the elbows than a hand's breadth.

The bridle must be adjusted in such a way that is does not constrict or rub the horse; the bit must not hurt it or be too tight against the corners of its mouth. The throat latch should be tightened only to the extent that one can easily insert a flat hand between it and the horse's throat. Any form of bridlery that hurts the horse affects adversely its capacity for obedience.

The bit used with a snaffle should be appropriate to the horse's degree of sensitivity. The thicker the bit, the gentler will be its effect and therefore the more sensitive the horse, the thicker will be the chosen bit. One will try to select the thickest possible bit for a young horse.

The dropped noseband gives a better seating for the bit and makes it more difficult for the horse to evade it by opening its mouth (see illustration 23).

The curb bit must suit the width of the horse's mouth, something which varies greatly. The finer the horse's head (as with thoroughbreds and Arabs), the narrower must be the mouthpiece of the curb bit; the larger the horse's head, the wider will be its mouth and the mouthpiece must be correspondingly wider. The more sensitive the horse's mouth, the shorter should be the curb cheeks, for the curb is, in effect, a lever, the severity of which is increased the longer the cheek of the curb below the mouthpiece. When the reins hang down, the curb cheeks should be in the same line of direction as the horse's mouth and there should be enough room to insert two fingers easily between curb chain and lower jaws. On taking up the reins, the cheeks should turn through about thirty degrees. If they turn more than this, or cannot be turned to this extent, the bit has been adjusted incorrectly.

AUXILIARY REINS

There are several different kinds of auxiliary reins:

1   Side-reins. These are fitted between the ring of the snaffle and the saddle girth. The horse is tightly reined when its nose is pulled in behind the vertical line so that its mouth is brought back towards its breast and loosely reined when the line of its forehead remains in front of the vertical line. Apart from lungeing (p. 189), one will not use side-reins in dressage work, for they are fixed and can only act rigidly. They are useful in giving instruction to a beginner who has yet to acquire a sense of balance.

2   Standing martingale. This can be used to make head-shaking more difficult in the case of fiery jumping horses. It can also replace side-reins in the instruction of beginners. This is only a single rein, unlike the side-reins, which runs from the girth between the front legs and is attached to the cavesson noseband and does not prevent lateral flexion.

3   Running martingale. This consists of a strap divided into two for some part of its length with the single part attached to the girth and running forward between the horse's front legs to be secured at each of its two ends by rings through which the snaffle reins pass. The single end may be attached alternatively to the breastplate. The martingale should be adjusted with adequate length to ensure that, when the reins are taken up, it hangs in a curve. The intention is not to prevent a horse shaking its head or raising it in the air but to restrict such actions so that the rider keeps control at such times, and runs less risk of being struck in the face by the horse's head. (Illustration 95 on p. 176 shows Hans Günter Winkler riding a horse with a properly adjusted martingale.)

The martingale has no application in dressage schooling. Its main usefulness lies

in jumping, hunting and perhaps in hacking
out on high-spirited horses.

4   The running-rein. This consists of two
    straps approximately 2.75 metres long. The
    end of each is buckled to the girth at roughly
    the height of the rider's knees. The straps
    are then taken forward and lead from the
    inside to the outside through the snaffle
    rings and into the rider's hands, the left-
    hand rein into the rider's left hand and the
    right-hand rein into his right hand. The
    rough surface of the straps should face the
    horse's body so that the smooth part of the
    leather can slip easily through the snaffle
    rings and lessen friction (see illustration 37,
    p. 94).

The running-rein must be used with great
care, for the real danger exists that, if it is
used too roughly, the horse's head is pulled
towards its chest and it should be used only
by those riders who have a requisite degree
of sensitivity, who know how a horse reacts
which is listening to the aids and who understand how, on such a horse, one can, as it
were, push a horse's head forward as if it
were at the end of two stiff rods. The
running-rein represents a misleading way of
achieving a flexed position with the hands
without the horse having been driven
forward into the bit, i.e. with collection.

In short, the running-rein should be used
only in conjunction with adequate forward-
driving influences and then only for those
brief periods when a horse shows resistance
by stiffness in its neck, poll and lower jaw.
The horse can be induced to yield by the
application of minimal pressure of the
outside hand while the inside hand is prepared to move forward slightly. We have
already described the method of teaching a
horse to stretch its head and neck forward
and downward on page 93. The important
point is that the running-rein must be used
with emphasis on one side, not with both
reins. When this unilateral rein use is found
to be effective on one side of the horse, this

may be attributed to the fact that one is not seeking for effect on the other side. And once the horse has learned to yield to both hands, there is no longer any point in continuing to use the running-rein.

Should one endeavour to use the running-rein to force a horse into a certain position or condition of flexion, one is acting in a manner that is totally contradicatory to true dressage principles. Resistance will be the inevitable consequence. When one does make use of running-reins, success should be achieved in a very few minutes. If it is not, the conclusion is that the rider does not understand their use and would be advised to discard them, as he will only compound his problems.

5 The chambon. This is an auxiliary rein intended, like the running-rein, to induce the horse to stretch its head and neck forward and downward. It is used mainly when lungeing and demands a skilful practitioner. One sees it being used to school a jumping horse over cavaletti, when it can be useful. While the running-rein acts on a horse that evades by putting pressure on its lower jaw and encourages it to bend at the poll, the chambon affects the horse's mouth; the higher the horse raises its head, the greater the pressure. The horse quickly learns that it can lessen this pressure by lowering its head and is thus encouraged to stretch its neck forward and downward. It must be borne in mind, however, and this applies to all aspects of rein influencing, that forward momentum must be maintained so that the horse does not end up standing almost on its head.

We must finally make the point that auxiliary reins may be of some small benefit in lightening the task of schooling a horse, but they can never begin to take the place of essential work a rider does in influencing effectively a horse that is totally obedient to the aids. They must be regarded only as minor fringe benefits.

BANDAGES

Bandages are put on a horse to protect its tendons. More often than not, their value is over-estimated. It does, however, happen that horses hurt themselves with their own shoes, usually when making tight turns, through stumbling, when jumping and so on, and such injuries may lead to splints (bone swellings) causing lameness. Certainly bandages are some protection against such knocks and provide support against sprains. Bandages must be put on very carefully. There must be no creases in them and, in fact, clumsy bandaging can cause damage. The ends of a bandage should be secured on the outside of the leg and pressure should not be so great as to cause damage. The knot should not be over a tendon and must be secure enough not to come undone in the course of a ride. If a bandage should come undone, a horse could easily put a foot on it and fall. To avoid this, bandages are often finally secured with adhesive tape over the knot.

When jumping or hunting, brushing boots are recommended as these give special protection against external injuries and cannot come loose.

Over-reach boots protect the heels and coronary bands and injuries to these could lead to a horse being out of action for lengthy periods of time.

SHOEING

This is a wide-ranging subject that is outside the scope of this book. We must content ourselves with a few salient points.

It is essential to inspect a horse's hooves daily. Only a skilled blacksmith who is available regularly can ensure that a horse's hooves are always in good condition. The decision whether a horse needs shoeing is dependent on the nature of the terrain and the relative strength of the horse's hooves. If there is any shadow of doubt, the horse should be shod. Calkins should only be put on the hooves of a healthy horse for a limited period of time for a specific purpose, after which they must be removed immediately.

Items in schooling

THE VOICE

An item that a rider can always use is his voice. It can be used to rouse or calm a horse. But just as one must use spurs and whip with consideration, so one should use the voice. A deep, kindly tone of voice has a soothing effect, while a strong, clear command can stimulate.

There should never be any loud shouting in the horse's box.

THE LUNGE

This is used to work a horse from the ground. It is a tape or webbing of approximately seven metres in length and is held in the left hand when the horse is to go round on the left rein, and in the right hand when on the right rein. The lunge is secured to the ring provided on the cavesson and this latter piece of equipment is well nigh indispensable for work from the hand, certainly with young horses, as otherwise the lunge could be too harsh for tender mouths. If a cavesson is not available, the lunge may be attached to the inside ring of the snaffle. The other end of the lunge and the last two or three metres – depending on the diameter of the circle – are held in the hand of the person carrying out the lungeing. He must take care that he does not allow the lunge to go slack to the extent that it might form coils that he could step in, and he should hold the lunge in his hand in such a way that he can pay it out or shorten it.

The controlling hand should be level with the horse's mouth and should seek to keep the lunge taut. Attempting to carry out lungeing with arm and lunge hanging down may make the horse move but cannot be called lungeing.

Lungeing is used in the initial schooling of a young horse, to accustom a green horse to the weight of a saddle, to teach jumping, to correct faults in problem horses, to help horses with weak backs whose riders are insufficiently skilled to harmonise their movements with those of the horse and also in the rehabilitation of horses who

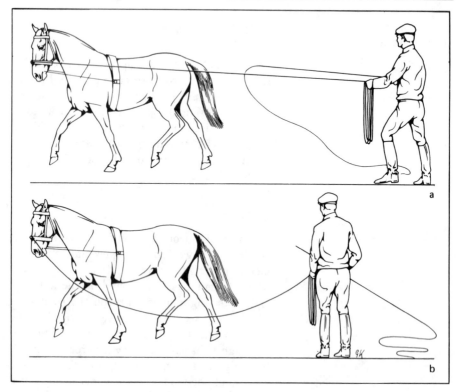

96 Lungeing:
a: Correct.
b: Wrong.

have lost their paces and impulsion through being ridden badly and in schooling horses who need gentle building-up after illness or injury.[1]

Lungeing is being properly carried out when a horse displays calm, energetic paces, but badly carried out if the horse is made to display an unnatural outline. It is essential correctly to adjust the side-reins and to make skilful and simultaneous use of lunge, whip and voice. These last two replace the influences that would normally be supplied by the rider's back and legs, while the varying action of the lunge together with the restraining side-reins take over the function of the rider's reins. The adjustment of these, as well as the correct use of voice and whip, demand skill, understanding and certainly concentration. The adjustment of the reins may well have

[1]Impulsion is not synonymous with pace or action. The term 'pace' refers to the extent of the stride or degree of elevation, while 'impulsion' is used to refer to the harmonious swinging movement with which the horse propels itself.

to be altered in the course of the work. Lungeing is, in fact, a far harder business than is generally assumed.

It needs to be stated that riders who cannot accommodate themselves to their horse's movements cannot make rectifications by lungeing their horse, for once they get back on the horse, it will very quickly suffer again as it did before. The only long-term remedy is that one applies oneself to the task of learning to go with the horse's movements until mastery is achieved.

CAVALETTI

Cavaletti are poles approximately three metres long, supported at the ends by cross-pieces, which can be turned to three different heights. In making the horse traverse them (with a rider on its back) either at walk or trot, one achieves the following:

1 The horse is obliged to pay attention to what it is stepping over and will take higher steps. If its rider does not interfere with it, it will usually stretch its neck forward and downward and relax its back muscles. One can also lunge a horse over cavaletti without a rider.

One should not ask too much of the horse, particularly if it tends to get excited or has a weak back, and care should be taken that the poles are not easily moved, the danger then being that, if they are dislodged, the distances will be wrong for any horse that is following as a class ride and more harm is done than good.

2 The rider can verify that he himself is relaxed and is accommodating himself to his horse's movements. He should take more grip with his knees in order to preclude getting behind his horse's movement and to avoid jabbing it in the mouth and thumping down on its back.[1]

[1]See 'Forward seat', pp. 41 and 140.

Cavaletti work is recommended for horses with a short, thickset back to loosen them and also for horses who have been badly ridden and, as a consequence, tense their back muscles and take irregular steps.

However, the value of cavaletti work tends to be over-estimated. A horse will certainly stretch its neck forward and downward but this does not help to give a rider insight into the way in which his own aids will accomplish this. In fact, he might as well watch his horse stretching its neck at the feeding trough for all the positive knowledge he will gain.